Happiness often sneaks in a door

you did not think was open...

Date Your Mate:
How to Save Your Marriage from "The Blahs" And Live Happily Ever After

Kalen Hammann, Ph.D.
("Dr. K")

Copyright © 2016 Kalen Hammann. All rights reserved.

No portion of this book may be reproduced in any manner whatsoever—mechanically, electronically, or by any other means, including photocopying or recording, or by any information storage and retrieval system—without written permission of the author, except in the case of brief quotations embedded in articles and reviews.

Published by:
New Pathways Publishers
2922 Rosemary Drive
Largo Fl. 33770

1-727-733-2178

www.DrKOnline.com

ISBN: 978-1-890002-18-3 (mobi/KDP)
ISBN: 978-1-890002-19-0 (ePub)
ISBN: 978-1-890002-20-6 (Paperback)

Limits of Liability/Disclaimer: The authors and/or publisher do not guarantee that anyone following the techniques, suggestions, tips, ideas, or strategies will have success. The reader assumes all responsibility and liability of the use of the information contained herein. Under no circumstances will Kalen Hammann ("Dr. K"), New Pathways Publishers, or any of their representatives or contractors be liable for any special or consequential damages that result from the use of, or the inability to use, the materials, information, or strategies communicated through these materials, or any services following these materials, even if advised of the possibility of such damages. The author and/or publisher shall have neither liability nor responsibility to anyone with respect to any loss or damage caused, or alleged to be caused, directly or indirectly by the information contained in this book. This book is not a substitute for professional counseling.

For Kari

*I wasn't sure for a while
that "Happily Ever After" was in the cards.
Thanks for hanging in there until we could make some real
progress toward learning what it takes!*

I love you.

PLEASE NOTE: FREE BONUS MATERIALS!

I HAVE PROVIDED BONUS MATERIALS ONLINE TO HELP YOU APPLY WHAT YOU WILL LEARN IN THIS BOOK TO YOUR OWN RELATIONSHIP.

CHECK OUT YOUR FREE BONUS MATERIALS NOW AT www.drkonline.com/dymbonus.

Table of Contents

FORWORD
  Are "The Blahs" Killing Your Marriage?

CHAPTER ONE 13
  What Do You Mean, "Save my marriage?"

CHAPTER TWO 21
  How to End the Cold War

CHAPTER THREE 27
  The ABC's of Living Happily Ever After

CHAPTER FOUR 30
  A Is for "Appreciation," "Attention" and "Affection"

CHAPTER FIVE 40
  Habit Gravity and Escape Velocity -
  How to Build a New Habit and Rewire Your Brain

CHAPTER SIX 44
  "Thank you for taking out the garbage!"

CHAPTER SEVEN 48
  Sawubona

CHAPTER EIGHT 54
How to Beat the Hidden Myth That Kills Relationships

CHAPTER NINE 62
B Is for "Break the Routine"

CHAPTER TEN 67
Where Did THAT Come From?

CHAPTER ELEVEN 76
"Our equipment isn't working right"

CHAPTER TWELVE 84
Getting Your Intelligence Back

CHAPTER THIRTEEN 91
C Is for "Create a Good Feeling"

CHAPTER FOURTEEN 94
A Carillon Playing Chopin?!

CHAPTER FIFTEEN 100
"You're special!"

CHAPTER SIXTEEN 104
  "Talk to me!"

CHAPTER SEVENTEEN 110
  Bang Bang Shrimp: the Power of Rituals

CHAPTER EIGHTEEN 117
  Something to Look Forward to

CHAPTER NINETEEN 120
  "One more thing. . ."

CHAPTER TWENTY 122
  "Surprise!"

CHAPTER TWENTY-ONE 126
  I Hope This Isn't the End!

CHAPTER TWENTY-TWO..129
  Afterword: "But what about. . ."

CHAPTER TWENTY-THREE...132
  "Don't Get Mad. . . Get Curious!" Sample Chapter

FOREWORD

Are "The Blahs" Killing Your Marriage?

Once upon a time, a boy was born.

A little earlier—or maybe it was a little later, I'm not really sure—a girl was born.

The boy grew up. The girl grew up.

It wasn't always easy, but after overcoming many difficulties, they found each other. They married.

And they lived happily ever after.

Sounds like a fairy tale, doesn't it?

Well, it's *not* a fairy tale!

There are people—thousands of couples—living happily ever after right now. We just don't hear much about them.

Mostly we hear the dismal statistics that more than half of all marriages end in divorce. That another 20-25% of couples aren't happy together.

But think about what that has to mean. It means that as many as 25% of couples *ARE* happy together!

It makes you wonder: *What do they know that the other couples don't know?*

For most of my life, I've been trying to find out. I sought the answer for years, until I learned about some groundbreaking research and all the pieces of the puzzle fell into place. I finally knew . . . But I'm getting ahead of my story. First let's talk about *your* relationship. . .

Remember how great things were when you were first dating?

You were so happy! You felt so ALIVE! You could hardly wait to see this magical person. You couldn't believe how lucky you were to be together.

When is the last time you felt that way about your mate? Weeks or months ago? Years?

Do you sometimes find yourself wondering, "What happened? Did I make a mistake? Was I dreaming? What happened to the wonderful person I thought I married? Sometimes this is relationship feels so DEAD. Sometimes it is so awful.

"Should I leave? Just call it quits, get out of this marriage, and start over?"

What turns newlywed bliss into a divorce waiting to happen?

It's as if over the days and weeks after the honeymoon a dark cloud gathers, and then sucks the life out of far too many relationships. I call that cloud "The Blahs."

Before you give up and walk out of your marriage—or quit trying and just resign yourself to settling for a marriage that isn't really what you want—you need to know one thing: even though The Blahs are so common that they affect nearly all relationships from time to time, *it can take remarkably little to save any marriage from The Blahs.*

Even yours.

CHAPTER ONE

What Do You Mean, "Save my marriage?"

(Author's note: throughout this book I'll be writing as though you're married, and married to someone of the opposite sex, but these same principles will help you save ANY relationship, whether from falling apart or simply from being the kind of "so-so" relationship you feel you're stuck with but don't really want to settle for. By the way, that includes relationships with your kids or even—with a few modifications!—with your boss, your co-workers, or your employees. I'll leave it up to you to make any needed translations.)

Maybe you know that your marriage needs saving. Your partner has walked out, or suggested a trial separation. Or you have been on the verge of doing the same thing. Or you're only staying together for the kids. Or you're afraid to leave—afraid of the unknown. Or, worst of all, because even though you know it's bad, you have decided, "This is just the way marriage is. It wouldn't be any better with anyone else. So I just have to put up with it!"

Maybe you'd say things are "OK," but you still feel something isn't right. Something important is missing. It's not what you expected, what you hoped for when you got together.

Either way, no matter what troubles you've gone through, no matter how things are now between you and your mate, *you can learn to do the few simple things the happy couples do.* Then you too will have a real shot at living happily ever after.

This book is here to point the way.

> (**PLEASE NOTE:** If your mate becomes so violent that you are physically injured, or you feel that your safety or that of a child is in danger, you probably need more help than this book can provide. Please search on the Internet for "Abuse hotline" and use the resources there to connect with someone you can talk with about your situation and what you need to do. DO IT TODAY, PREFERABLY RIGHT NOW! After you've done that, you can continue. We'll wait. :-)

Let me tell you a little about how this book came to be.

Imagine being four years old, and being waked up in the middle of the night. . .

> *I was living in Yakima, Washington. The day before, I had eaten my first peach, grown right there. It was the most delicious thing I had ever tasted. My dad was away on a business trip. I was sound asleep when my mom shook me gently awake, saying, "It's time to go." I was excited, but a little scared, too. I didn't know where we were going or why we had to leave in the middle of the night.*
>
> *My mom took the bags she had packed and my younger sister Clare and me to the train station.*
>
> *We traveled halfway across the country, to Chicago, where my grandparents lived. We weren't going for a visit. Sometime during the journey my mom called my dad and told him she wanted a divorce. . .*
>
> *For the next several weeks I heard her side of telephone conversations with my dad. They mostly included my mother saying things like, "Art, I don't know why you keep banging your head against a brick wall. It's over."*

My dad had been completely blindsided. I remember him coming to visit a couple of years later and just sitting on a hillside, crying...
He never really understood why she had left. It's not that she didn't try to tell him. But he never understood.

It was hard for me to understand, too. For a long time it just didn't make sense to me that two intelligent, well-meaning people who had loved each other enough to get married couldn't make it together. He was a good guy, caring and funny. There was never any abuse or anything like that. He was obviously crazy about her.

But love was not enough.

Why not? What would it have taken to save their marriage?

Why is love not enough?

I wondered about it for years.

Eventually, my questions led me to the University of Michigan, where I got a doctorate in social psychology, and to Esalen Institute in California and training programs elsewhere focused on various ways of evoking and nurturing human potential like Gestalt Therapy, Family Therapy, and est. I learned some things I thought could help people build better lives and better relationships and began working with people in the Boston area as a licensed psychologist.

Some of the approaches I had learned did seem to help some people, but not as consistently as I would have liked. Too often, the tools I had developed didn't work for the people who needed them most. I didn't feel I really knew what I was doing or what was really needed.

I shifted direction, got trained to lead seminars in building successful business relationships, and began working with business leaders and managers all around the world, helping them learn how to empower their workers, do win-

win negotiating, and build cross-cultural teams. The techniques people learned seemed to be useful, but I still felt something essential was missing.

I began to study brain science, and started to get some new insights about what goes wrong in relationships and how to set it right.

Then I ran across the work of John Gottman. That was when all the pieces of the puzzle fell into place.

Happily ever after

Dr. Gottman, it turned out, has been doing remarkable research on couple relationships for decades. He began by videotaping ordinary people as they talked about their day, things they disagreed about, and so on while they were hooked up to apparatus that could measure their physiological responses like heart rate, breathing, blood flow, and even how much they squirmed in their chairs. He went on to videotape them while they spent a full day together in a small apartment, doing whatever they did on an average Sunday.

Amazingly, Dr. Gottman didn't have any theory he was trying to prove or disprove. He just wanted to see what happened. He followed up with the couples for several years to see how they were doing, and that was when the important part of the research took place. After a while, as you would expect, some of the couples divorced. Others stayed together, but when Dr. Gottman asked them, they admitted that they weren't really happy together. Still others WERE happy together—their marriages weren't perfect, but they actually became happier and more satisfied as the years passed.

I was very excited when I learned this. For years I had been hearing the dismal statistics that almost half, then half, then *more* than half of marriages were ending in divorce. I had begun to wonder if all marriages were just divorces waiting to happen. Maybe my parents had just realized it earlier than some and bowed to the inevitable.

But I realized that Dr. Gottman's research told another story. There *are* some truly happy marriages out there. It's not a myth: *some couples really do live happily ever after!*

Then Dr. Gottman went back to the videotapes he had taken when the couples were newlyweds to see if he could tell what made the difference—what the couples who ended up happy together did differently from the others. And he made an amazing discovery.

The discovery that changes everything

Dr. Gottman found that he could watch a videotape of a couple for as little as 5 or 10 minutes and predict whether they would end up happy together, unhappy together, or divorced—with over 90% accuracy!

If you know anything about psychology, you know that NOTHING in psychology is 90%. If a psychologist can find a correlation of 15 or 20% he counts himself very fortunate, and happily publishes the results. To be able to predict not just what ONE person will do, but what TWO people will do years later with over 90% accuracy is practically unheard of.

It turns out that *couples who stay together happily do a few simple things that other couples don't do.*

Besides being curious about what those "few simple things" are, I immediately thought, as I imagine you may be thinking, "This is all very nice, but can couples for whom it doesn't come naturally to do what the happy couples do LEARN to do it? And if they do, will it make a difference in their relationships?"

The answers, you will be happy to learn, as I was, are "Yes" and "Yes." Yes, people who don't "naturally" do what happy couples do can learn to do these things. Even better, yes, when people do learn to create these new habits, their relationships change for the better. We know this because Dr. Gottman, ever the researcher, has tested it out.

There's more!

As I learned from Dr. Gottman's research about what happy couples do that other couples don't do, I was excited because I saw that this research provided some missing pieces to the puzzle I'd been putting together over the years as I built a picture of what it takes to have a successful, satisfying, happy relationship. I also saw that I had some additional pieces from the other work and thinking I had been doing. When I put all those pieces together, I knew I had something simple but powerful: a set of principles and practices that people could use immediately to change their marriages and their lives. I immediately tested them in my own marriage and in sessions with the couples who came to see me professionally. They work!

I wrote this book to help you learn those principles and practices and use them to save your marriage and build the relationship you've always wanted. (And to help other people you know who may need them—so please help me make sure they hear about these practices and habits by passing the word!)

No matter how many books you read on learning to swim, the only way to learn is to get in the water. If you really want to improve a relationship, don't just read this book. Get busy applying the ideas you will learn about.

I have three suggestions that can help you to get the most out of reading this book. First, read any parts of it that you find helpful aloud to your partner—or suggest that he or she read them. Or read the whole book aloud with your mate!

Second, make notes of ideas you have as you read of things you want to try doing to bring more happiness to your relationship. (I've included a few pages at the end of the book where you can do that.)

Third, when I let you know there are bonus materials waiting for you online, take a moment to download those materials—and then put them to use! Every day, put some of what you are reading and thinking about into practice.

If you like, you can download all the bonus materials now so you'll have them ready when you come to them in the book. Remember, they're a free bonus—you can get them at www.drkonline.com/dymbonus.

Coming attractions

Here's what you can look forward to as you read this book:

In the next chapter you will learn the simplest, most powerful principle I know—a way to get free immediately from any morass in which you feel stuck, in your relationship or anywhere else in your life.

Then you'll learn why most relationships begin so wonderful and then go downhill so fast.

You'll learn the ABC's of relationship—what you can do every day to make your relationship better than the day before, starting today!

You will learn why it is so hard to deal with those times when things are NOT wonderful—why small annoyances or unkind, thoughtless remarks so often escalate into major blowups or icy silence—and how to deal with those times more gracefully.

You'll learn to recognize the myth that kills thousands of relationships—and the kernel of truth behind the myth that can take *your* relationship to a whole new level.

You will learn how busyness and the daily routine can turn a vital, alive relationship into a treadmill we plod along, living parallel lives with little real connection—and what you can do at any moment to get the good feeling back.

You'll learn why most good intentions go nowhere—why you are likely *not* to benefit much from what you're reading here unless you make use of a simple way to multiply the impact of everything else you do.

And you'll learn why the title of this book is Date Your Mate!

All aboard!

Now you know where this train—or maybe rocket—is headed, so let's get started.

The first principle—the way to get unstuck any time you feel trapped in a situation that is going downhill fast—is something I learned from Tony Robbins and Mikhail Gorbachev. (And Judy Carlberg.)

CHAPTER TWO

How to End the Cold War

When I was a child, something adults called "the cold war" somehow made the world a very dangerous place. We lived under the shadow of imminent nuclear war. If someone miscalculated just a little, the nuclear bombs could rain down all over the United States and the Soviet Union, and other places too, and we would all be dead.

Sometimes when I heard the whistle of a plane heading to the airport nearby I would be afraid it was an incoming nuclear bomb. My palms would sweat and my heart would race. It would take a while for me to calm down and get over being scared.

Amazingly, with all the dangers we face today, THAT threat is no longer with us.

How did this happen? What changed? How could we have been headed down a path leading to total destruction and then change course?

And why are we talking about this, anyway?

We're talking about it because *what stopped the cold war might help you save your marriage.*

I was at a workshop led by Tony Robbins called Date With Destiny led by Tony Robbins. Tony's lifelong quest has been, as he puts it, to find "strategies and tools that can immediately change the quality of people's lives." At the workshop, Tony told us that he had been wondering what stopped the cold war. Now of course the answer is complicated, involving geo-political strategies, economic forces, sociological and psychological factors, and a lot more.

But Tony realized that a key part of the answer had to do with a shift in the relationship between two men: Mikhail Gorbachev, the new leader of the Soviet Union, and Ronald Reagan, the president of the United States. Tony wanted to know how that shift had occurred. He set out to learn the answer from one of the two men involved—Mikhail Gorbachev.

Tony can be very creative, and also very persistent. Eventually he was sitting across from Mr. Gorbachev (in a plane he had chartered specifically to give Mr. Gorbachev a ride to a meeting where he would be speaking!). And Tony asked the question he had been wondering about.

> *"I know that the end of the cold war had a lot to do with your relationship with President Reagan. How did your relationship with President Reagan change from one of enmity to one where you could help each other to build a better, safer world for all of us?"*
>
> Tony described what happened next: *"Mr. Gorbachev said something about how they had just gradually gotten to know each other better and more and more came to trust each other. I said, 'NO. That's not the way it happened. I know how these things work. There was a MOMENT at some point when things changed forever. Tell me about that moment!'"*
>
> *"Mr. Gorbachev looked a bit taken aback. Then he slapped his knee and said, 'That is a very good question! No one has ever asked me that question before. You are a very good interviewer! Let me think about it.' He thought for a moment. Then he began to speak."*
>
> *"It was the first time I met your President Reagan. After the pleasantries, we began to talk seriously. He began lecturing me about the evils of communism. And I began lecturing him*

right back about the evils of capitalism. We both felt strongly about what we were saying. It was a very intense conversation.

"We began to become angry. Our voices were getting louder and louder.

"Suddenly Mr. Reagan stopped and stood up. Then he turned away.

"I was shocked. I thought he was leaving! I never expected what happened next.

"Mr. Reagan turned back to face me with a big smile on his face and said, 'Let's begin again. My name is Ron. May I call you Mikhail?'

"In that moment, I knew that I could work with this man. From that moment, everything changed."

And because the course of that conversation changed, the relationship between two world leaders changed. The relationship between two great nations changed. And the world changed—for all of us.

"Do-Over!"

I told that story in a workshop I was leading, to illustrate that no matter how bad a relationship has become, there is always the possibility that we can begin again. We can build a new, far more satisfying relationship together.

Judy Carlberg, one of the workshop participants, spoke up. (I'll bet you've been wondering, "Who is Judy Carlberg?" Now you know. :-)

"That's what my husband Ladd and I do," Judy said. We call it a Do-Over,

"What's a Do-Over," I asked.

"It's like when we were kids playing softball or something and people disagreed about whether somebody who tried to steal a base was safe or out. There was no referee, so

somebody called a Do-Over and we just started again from where we were before she tried to steal the base.

"That's what Ladd and I do when we get into an argument and start getting mad at each other. One of us just says 'Do-Over!' We stop and look at each other. Sometimes we just burst out laughing and the tension is broken, and we go on talking calmly and peacefully.

"Other times we're still mad. Then one of us will go out of the room and come back in with a smile and a cheery hello. The other one grins and we go on from there. It nearly always works!"

Amazing!

Even though I'd gotten the general point of Tony's story about Mr. Reagan and Mr. Gorbachev—that even the most difficult, potentially destructive relationship can be turned around if we're willing to simply begin again—until Judy said that I hadn't thought of using this as a way to turn a conversation around if it's headed over a cliff.

But I've tried it since, and every time the experience has been amazing.

For me, it seems to work best to do a combination of what Mr. Reagan did and what Judy and Ladd do:

> *When I notice that a conversation with my wife Kari is starting to go off the rails, I say, "Could we begin again?" Then without waiting for an answer, I turn around and leave the room. I come back in saying something positive that starts the conversation we had been having from a different, more positive place.*
>
> *Let's say Kari has mentioned how I left a bunch of dishes out the night before instead of putting them in the dishwasher before coming to bed. (Putting the dishes in the dishwasher is one of the things I usually do, because I know Kari likes to come in to a clean kitchen in the morning). When Kari*

mentions the dishes I start getting defensive and try to explain that we had left for a movie right after dinner and then gotten back so late I just wanted to get to bed and I simply forgot. She starts talking about other times I "forgot" to do things we agreed I would do, and I get more defensive and begin bringing up things SHE hasn't done, and—you can see where this is heading.

As soon as I notice what's happening—mainly by feeling my stomach and my jaw getting tight—I'll say, "This isn't going anywhere good. Can we begin again?"

Then I go out and come back into the room saying, with a smile, "You know, something just occurred to me. After the movie last night I left some dishes out. I'm sorry—I know that was a hassle for you."

Maybe she'll just say, "No big deal. Thanks for noticing" and grin. Maybe she'll say, "Yes, what can we do next time we go out right after dinner so that won't happen again?" Either way, our conversation will work out better than it would have before the Do-Over.

What is amazing is how different I FEEL as soon as we begin again.

I know the principle involved: *what we feel depends on what we are focusing on.* Think about what happens when two people are in an argument and the phone rings. As soon as one person answers the phone, you can immediately see the person's face and breathing and body language and tone of voice change. As the person's focus shifts, so do their feelings.

But even though I know the principle, it's still amazing to feel how powerful this is.

Try it yourself!

You won't really know how powerfully beginning again can impact your own relationship until you try it.

So try it!

When you have that sinking feeling—or angry feeling—that a conversation is going nowhere good, STOP!

In a neutral or friendly tone, say, "Let's begin again!"

If you can, smile and say something friendly.

If you can't quite manage that, physically turn away or leave the room for just a moment. Shift your focus and reconnect with your best self.

Then come back ready to make a good connection and determined to have a positive conversation.

More often than not, the other person will relax and join you!

It can change everything when you notice that a conversation is going downhill and realize you can simply begin again.

But what if you don't just want to change the course of a conversation? What if you want to change the whole course your relationship is on?

And why do we need to begin again in the first place?

CHAPTER THREE

The ABC's of Living Happily Ever After

Nearly every marriage (except for some arranged marriages or marriages of convenience) begins with two people so much in love that they want to spend the rest of their lives together.

Just a few years later, half of them are heading for the divorce court. And many of the others are unhappy together, hanging in there with no real hope that things will ever be any better. They figure they just have to "get used to it."

Well, after working with couples who were probably more convinced than you are that there was no hope that their relationship could ever really improve, I can tell you this: you don't have to get used to a so-so relationship.

You just need to know what actually happens that kills so many marriages.

***Please note:** As I mentioned in Chapter 1, there is one group of marriages that the principles and practices in this book probably WON'T save: marriages where there is serious abuse, whether physical, emotional, sexual, whatever. If that's your situation, my strong advice is, call a hotline—search on Google for "abuse hotline"—and get help making a plan that will keep you safe. Once you're out of this situation, you can use what you'll learn here to make your next relationship really great!*

What happens is very simple. *Most people stop doing the things they were doing when they were dating and start doing other things instead.*

Why does this matter? Because the things most people naturally do when they are dating are perfectly designed to bring out the best in themselves and each other. We don't intentionally or consciously do them for that reason, but that's the effect they have.

That's why the early days and weeks of a relationship can be such a magical time—and why, being our best and seeing the best in this other person, we fall in love.

After the honeymoon, most couples stop doing the things that brought out the best in themselves and each other when they were dating. Instead, they often start doing what brings out the worst!

When they do, their partners seem to change into someone else. Someone a lot less attractive.

And things go downhill from there. All too soon, they can begin to wonder what they ever saw in this person. Or think, "Whatever happened to the person I fell in love with?"

Some couples, on the other hand, keep doing what they were doing when they were dating. And their marriages flourish.

What are the things the happy couples do?

I call them *the ABC's of living happily ever after.*

A is for *Appreciation*—and also for *Attention* and *Affection*.

B is for *Break the routine*—and also for *Brain transplant!*

C is for *Create a good feeling*. This is the key to bringing a dead or dying (or anemic) relationship back to life. You might think it would happen naturally. But it doesn't!

For a free down-loadable poster, "The ABC's Of Living Happily Ever After," go to www.drkonline.com/dymbonus.

Want a few more details? Let's begin with "A."

CHAPTER FOUR

A is for "Appreciation," "Attention" and "Affection"

A pair of researchers observed couples spending an average evening at home. As they watched, they noted on clipboards each time one of the partners spoke, noting what was said and whether the comment was "positive" ("Thanks for doing the dishes, Hon"), "negative" ("Are you watching that stupid program again? I don't know why you waste your time with that drivel!") or "neutral" ("The light bulb needs changing"). After a couple of hours the researchers asked each of the people they had been observing to make three lists: to write down everything they could remember that their partner had said that was positive, negative, and neutral.

Comparing the lists made by different couples, the researchers made a startling discovery.

Some couples remembered quite accurately everything their partners had said that was negative, but not most of the things their partners had said that was positive.

For other couples the reverse was true: they remembered most of their partners' positive comments, but not most of the negative ones.

In both cases, what they remembered as positive or negative matched well what the researchers had coded as positive or negative.

> *While it was interesting that couples differed in this way, what was most revealing about their relationships was something else.*
>
> *The couples who remembered mostly what their partner said that was negative also saw many items the two researchers had each considered "neutral" like 'The light bulb needs changing" or 'It looks like rain. You might want to take a raincoat when you go to the store" as NEGATIVE. When the researchers asked why, it turned out that the couples had seen the comments as a criticism or a put-down ("Does he think I'm too stupid to remember to wear a raincoat if it's raining?").*
>
> *The researchers described this pattern as "negative sentiment override." It was as if these couples were wearing colored glasses or listening through filters that put a negative spin on everything that happened.*
>
> *With other couples it was just the opposite. They experienced "positive sentiment override." Those who remembered more of their partner's positive comments also tended to see as POSITIVE many items the two researchers had considered neutral. Why? "When she said the light bulb needed changing, I felt good knowing that she didn't want me to strain my eyes by reading in inadequate light." "It's nice that he wanted to make sure I would stay dry if it was raining."*

It's pretty clear that the couples who "accentuate the negative"—without even knowing they're doing it—are having a much more unpleasant experience within their marriages than the others.

> *When we're dating, we're nearly always in "positive sentiment override."* We're so happy to be with the person we're dating, and we speak of them in such glowing terms that our friends may shake their heads and say we have stars in our eyes.

Maybe so. But that raises an interesting question.

Why do those stars fade?

The stars fade because after the honeymoon people begin noticing things about each other that are at first annoying and then gradually begin driving them crazy!

"You are such a . . . "

While you were dating, you were having a wonderful time getting to know each other. You were amazed and delighted by the differences between you.

But after the honeymoon you get focused on all the day-to-day activities that keep a house going. And at that point the differences that were "cute" begin to be exasperating. You have different ideas about how to get things done, different ideas about how to raise kids when they come along, even different ideas about how to drive safely. It begins to really bug you how your partner is always late, or always making such a big deal about getting everywhere early. Or how your partner is such a slob—or such a neat freak. Or how your partner never seems to be in the mood for sex—or is all over you even when you've had a rough day and just want to go to sleep.

Does this mean that we're simply becoming more realistic? Are we beginning to see our partners as they really are? If so, our marriages are surely doomed!

Fortunately, while we may be seeing new sides of our partners as we get to know them better, this isn't the root of the problem.

The root of the problem is a dynamic that operates beneath our awareness, coloring our whole experience of life:

Whatever you pay most attention to, you start seeing more and more of.

Where did all the babies come from?

Think about the last time you bought a car. Suddenly the roads were full of cars like the ones you were considering.

If you have a child, remember how in the weeks before your child was born the world was suddenly full of pregnant women and people walking with strollers?

Were all those cars and babies there before? Of course they were!

But until you started paying attention to them, you didn't notice them. It was as if they *weren't* there—for you.

So the more we begin to notice and pay attention to and think about things that we find frustrating or unpleasant or exasperating about our partner, the more things like that we see.

Besides that, the more your partner feels criticized and negatively judged, the more defensive or off balance he or she gets, and as that happens, more and more of your partner's negative qualities come out instead of the positive qualities you fell in love with.

Pretty soon you have a dismal outlook and are living in a downward spiral that feeds on itself. As that happens, you can develop a *habit* of seeing your partner in a negative light.

This is how it can get to the point where couples don't even notice many of the positive things their partner does, and interpret neutral comments ("The light bulb needs changing") as criticism or even an attack ("Can't you see I just got home? I can't do EVERYTHING the minute I walk in the door!").

Over time, people shift from lovers to roommates—then to annoying roommates who never seem to do their share of the chores or pull their share of the weight and are always complaining. Or they begin living parallel lives, keeping their distance to avoid setting off the next argument.

And that, too, becomes a habit. Like other habits, it gets wired into the brain, so it starts happening automatically. It becomes the path of least resistance for both people.

Usually it's no one's fault. It's just the way our brains are built.

There's something else about our brains that adds fuel to the fire.

We're Not Wired Right For Happiness!

We find it so easy to get into this kind of negative habit because of the way our brains are constructed. As one brain researcher puts it, "We're like Teflon for the positive and like Velcro for the negative." In other words, too often positive events just slip right by without our even noticing, while negative events stick with us like tenacious lint on a jacket and we dwell on them, going over and over them, making ourselves more and more unhappy. And as we do, the new path in our brains toward seeing our partner negatively becomes a superhighway.

Some people do this more than others, but we all have this tendency built into our brains.

Fortunately, though, that's not the end of the story.

We Can Change The Wiring!

Brain scientists are just beginning to appreciate how changeable our brains really are. Just as we can change a habit like driving on one side of the road if we move to another country, or learn to use our other hand to brush our teeth or even to write with if our dominant hand is injured, we can change our habitual ways of thinking.

Whenever we change a habit like this, we are first creating new pathways in our brains and then strengthening them.

It just takes a bit of conscious practice at doing things a new way instead of the way that comes "naturally." And then sticking with it until the new way becomes the new "natural." Once that happens, we know our brains have been rewired.

The old wiring doesn't go away. It's still available, like the old highway running alongside a new interstate. But now we have a choice about which way to go—a choice we didn't have before.

The Marriage Saver, Part I

Remember back when you were dating, how happy you were to see your partner each time you got together? Remember how good it felt to see your partner light up when you came into a room? You were both fully aware of what was wonderful about this other person, and you were each bathing in the other's appreciation. And you were eager to offer compliments.

That's part of the magic that makes dating so wonderful.

Couples who stay together happily—who live happily ever after with each other—keep that pattern going. Most people don't.

Whenever the happy couples have been separated, they take a moment to greet each other warmly.

On the other hand, after the honeymoon the couples who end up divorced or unhappy together are usually "too busy" or too distracted to even notice when their partner returns. At best they greet them with a perfunctory "Hi Hon," without being fully present.

This is a habit worth changing.

The results from making this one simple change can be so powerful that I call it The Marriage Saver (Part 1).

All it takes to create this new habit is to make a point of taking a moment to greet each other warmly every morning when you wake up, and every time you've been separated for awhile - like when you meet after one person or both have been away at work.

Greeting each other is pretty easy. But how do you manage the "warmly" part without pretending something you don't feel?

"How do I love thee? Let me count the ways..."

The reason we light up when we see our partner again while we're dating is that we're immediately reminded of the things we appreciate and love about them - their warmth, their looks, their smile, their sense of humor and upbeat attitude - whatever.

To greet *your* partner warmly, you just need to be thinking of things like that.

So part of The Marriage Saver is *to tell your partner one thing you appreciate or love about them each time you meet.*

It's ideal if you mention different things, but it's fine if you eventually repeat yourself. What's important is that you slow down enough that you actually FEEL how much you appreciate, like, or love what you are telling your partner about. "I love the sparkle in your eyes." "I like the way you look at me." "I really appreciate your strength."

The key is that you shift mental gears so you are fully present when you do it, focused on your partner instead of on what you were doing or what you're about to do.

So let's put these elements together.

The Marriage Saver (Part 1)

Any time you have been separated from your partner for a few hours or more—every morning you're in the same place, or when you get back together after work, etc. —do this:

Take a couple of moments to greet your partner.
Stop whatever else you're doing,
Forget or let go of what you were about to do next.
Be fully present with each other.
Feel how lucky you are, how fortunate you are to have this person in your life and to be together.
Tell your partner something you like or appreciate or love about them.

How will this help save our relationship?

This is the first step toward living in *positive sentiment override.* Remember, whatever you pay attention to, you will see more of. So when you spend a few minutes a day paying attention to what is special about your partner and how fortunate you are to be together, you'll begin to notice more and more good things about your partner.

Besides that, something wonderful happens when someone feels that another person appreciates them. They relax and feel better about themselves. As they do, more and more of their good qualities come to the surface and begin to show up in their lives.

So the more you appreciate your partner, the more reasons you will have to appreciate them! It's a virtuous cycle.

Before I suggest anything to someone else, I try it in my own marriage.

> *The morning after I made up The Marriage Saver, I greeted my wife Kari with a warm kiss. "Mmm, YOU'RE in a good mood!" she said with her eyes sparkling.*
>
> *I told her about my idea of taking a moment to really greet each other when we've been separated and telling each other something we appreciate about each other. "I really love your sparkling eyes," I said. "Well, I love the way you make up things to make our life better," she said, grinning. I felt wonderful. My day was off to a very good start!*

> *Because I often work out of an office in my home, I'm frequently in my office when Kari comes in the front door. When I heard the door open, I shouted, "Is that my Honey?" "Yes it is!" Kari called back. I got up, ran to greet her, gave her a hug, and said, "I love your voice!" She said, "you mean this isn't just in the morning?" I said, "Nope!" She said, "Well, I love your warmth—and your enthusiasm!"*

I felt so good I knew I had something.

I must tell you that after the novelty wore off, it took some energy to remember to do this—to make a special effort to greet each other when we've been apart.

But every time we do it, it gives our day and our marriage a boost.

> *If you're out of the habit of appreciating what is special about your partner or just want to deepen your appreciation so you have*

something to say when you greet each other, you can go right now to www.drkonline.com/dymbonus. You'll find an easy, enjoyable activity called "The Appreciation Builder."

Of course, you don't have to limit yourself to appreciating your partner when you greet each other. But before we talk about more ways you can appreciate your partner, let's take a moment to explore what it will take to make ANYTHING in this book work for you.

CHAPTER FIVE

*Habit Gravity and Escape Velocity -
How to Build a New Habit
and Rewire Your Brain*

(This chapter is brief, but it's critical for everything you will be learning in this book!)

If you want to save your marriage, you need to begin doing the "few simple things" the happy couples do not just a couple of times or once in a while, but *consistently*. You need to get to the point where you do them automatically, without thinking about it.

That means they have to become *habits*.

Habit Gravity and Escape Velocity

Eben Pagan (ebenpagan.com) has an online program called Wake Up Productive designed to help people at least double their productivity in 90 days. (It works!) In that program Eben describes why so many people start off to do something new and then find that it doesn't go anywhere.

He says that building a new habit is like launching a space shuttle. The shuttle sits on top of a huge rocket whose only purpose is to burn a great deal of fuel for a couple of minutes, get the shuttle moving fast enough to escape earth's gravity ("escape velocity") and then drop away, leaving the shuttle to use its own tiny engines to maneuver in space, do its job, and then come home.

In the same way, when we are building a new habit - trying to eat differently to lose weight, to begin an exercise routine, etc. —at first it can take a huge amount of energy to overcome the "gravity" of our usual way of doing things. If we aren't prepared for this, when our initial enthusiasm fades we will find that our old way of doing things takes over. We "don't feel like" doing the new habit we're trying to establish, we stop doing it, and we soon end up with the same old pattern instead of the benefits of the new habit we were trying to build.

When we ARE prepared for the pull of habit gravity, we will recognize our growing feeling that "this isn't worth the trouble" or even defiance ("Don't tell ME what to do. You can't make me!") for what they are: our old automatic ways of doing things trying to pull us back to earth. Instead of giving in to this "habit gravity," we will keep on pushing through the feelings until—it often only takes two or three weeks—we get over the hump and our new behavior begins to become easier and easier to do because it becomes a habit.

Soon we find that the new habit is in place and the new pattern is happening automatically, as a reflex, without our even thinking about it.

Psychologist William James said it even more simply (see next page):

How to change a habit
(By William James)

1. *Launch yourself with as strong and decided an initiative as possible*

2. *Never suffer an exception to occur till the new habit is securely rooted in your life.*

3. *Seize the very first possible opportunity to act on every resolution you make, and on every emotional prompting you may experience in the direction of the habits you aspire to gain. It is not in the moment of their forming, but in the moment of their producing motor effects, that resolves and aspirations communicate the new 'set' to the brain.*

To put it another way,

BEGIN AT ONCE
DO IT ENTHUSIASTICALLY
NO EXCEPTIONS!

Don't try to do too much at once!

One more thing: There's a growing body of research that suggests that will power is like a muscle. When we overuse our arm by lifting too many rocks building a stone wall, we may get so tired that we can't lift anything else until we rest.

So if we try to build too many new habits at once, it's easy to get overwhelmed and find all the new habits falling apart, and we end up right back where we started.

As we go through this book, I'm going to suggest developing a number of new habits that will help you make your relationship better and more satisfying. If at some point you begin to feel overwhelmed and find you're not doing ANY of the things I suggest, just remember this principle and go back to working on fewer habits—maybe only one—until it is solidly in place. Then you can go on to establish others.

The most powerful habit I know for improving a relationship is the habit you learned in the previous chapter: the Marriage Saver. So why not start with that?

Just be prepared to push through the habit gravity until you reach escape velocity and find that you're regularly greeting each other warmly, without even thinking about it.

With all this in mind, let's consider other ways you can expand the habit of appreciating your partner more and more.

CHAPTER SIX

"Thank you for taking out the garbage!"

Appreciation throughout the day (The Marriage Saver Part 2)

One of the ways "real life" is different from the special time of dating is that once we start living together there are all manner of small chores that need to be done to maintain our households. These chores provide a great opportunity to build positive sentiment that most people miss. We can use them to build the habit of noticing and appreciating good things about each other.

> When I first learned that couples who stay happy together appreciate each other more than those who don't, I began suggesting at my workshops that couples make a point of thanking each other for the small things each person does every day to help keep things running around the house. I had talked about this kind of thing occasionally with my wife Kari, but she hadn't really picked up on it. But then she sat in on one of my workshops, and our marriage changed.
> One of my jobs is emptying the kitchen trash into the big garbage can out in back of our house. I've been doing it for years—ever since we got married. But the next day, as I came back in with the empty kitchen trash can, Kari grinned and said, "Thanks for taking out the garbage."

I was amazed at how wonderful that felt!

A little later I thanked her for doing the grocery shopping as I carried the grocery bags in from the car—and she thanked me for the help. We both felt good.

Ever since, we've been thanking each other for little things like that—not every time, but frequently. Every time Kari thanks me, I get a little spark of pleasure.

And after even the first couple of weeks, I could feel the difference it was making. I had felt pretty good about our marriage before that, but suddenly I felt a new level of happiness when I thought of Kari and of our being together.

You might say, "Why should she thank you for taking out the garbage? That's your JOB!"

But that would be missing the point.

Everyone wants, likes, maybe even NEEDS to be appreciated. We may tell ourselves, "I shouldn't need that. I should just do what I'm supposed to do and not depend on someone's reaction to feel good about myself."

And it's true that we don't want our self-esteem to depend on another person's response.

But it feels so GOOD to be appreciated. Why?

First, when we do something day after day that someone else benefits from and NO appreciation is expressed, it's easy to begin feeling taken for granted. From there it's just a short step to feeling resentful—even like someone's slave.

A simple "thank you" can change all that.

On the other hand, we all want to feel that what we do *matters*, that it is making a positive difference in someone else's life. At some level every man wants to be his mate's knight in shining armor—to have his partner treasure the gifts he is giving, whether by slaying a dragon or taking out the garbage!

And every woman wants her partner to receive and value the gifts she is giving by the time and energy and love she puts into cooking a meal or managing daily finances.

Again a simple thank you can make all the difference. "Oh, she *got* it. She *values* what I did." "He *noticed*! It *touched* him."

And the feeling of closeness continues to build between them.

Beyond that, of course, by making a point of noticing and appreciating what your mate does, you are also building your own reservoir of good feeling about your mate and about the relationship. Together you are tipping the scales away from "Our relationship is just a series of hassles" toward "Our relationship is a series of moments of feeling close and cared for and grateful for being together."

That's the Marriage Saver Part II.

The Marriage Saver Part II

Throughout the day, whenever an opportunity arises, express appreciation.
Thank your partner for little things.
It doesn't have to be a big deal. Just let him/her know you noticed,
and that you feel good about what s/he did.

(Of course, if you want to, you could surprise your mate sometime with something that makes the "little thing" s/he did special—like a certificate naming your mate "The world's best garbage man" or "The world's best cook!")

There's No Need to Mention Everything

Although it feels good at first, it can come to seem like overkill to be thanking each other for every little thing throughout the day. And the last thing you want to do is to start feeling that you each "owe" your partner an expression of appreciation every time you do something to help keep the household running. Still, an occasional thank you will feel very good. At first, you'll do better to err on the side of overdoing it. You'll be able to tell if it's becoming too much.

There's one more way to build appreciation into your day that is a favorite with many of my clients. In addition to greeting each other warmly each morning, you can "bookend" your day with another appreciation time just before you go to bed. You'll find some suggestions on how to make it work best (I call it "The Marriage Saver, Part III") at <u>www.drkonline.com/dymbonus</u>.

Appreciation feels good, but it's important in another way too. Appreciation actually adds life to a relationship. A traditional Zulu greeting can help us understand why.

CHAPTER SEVEN

Sawubona

> The Zulu greeting, Sawubona, is sometimes translated as simply, "Hello." But it actually means, "I see you." Or even "We see you—my ancestors and I see you." The answer, "Ngikhona," means "I am here." The implication is that until you saw me, I didn't exist. By recognizing me, you brought me into existence. A Zulu folk saying expresses something like this: "Umuntu ngumuntu nagabantu," meaning "A person is a person because of other people."

"Pay attention to me!"

A is also for *Attention*

Part of the reason that appreciation feels so good is that it means someone else is paying attention to us and is aware of what we're doing.

We are social beings. For all of us, attention from another human being is like food for our souls.

> Babies in a nursery in World War II who were fed and kept warm and had their diapers changed but otherwise got no human attention withered. Many died. The babies in one ward who were regularly picked up and given loving attention, on the other hand, flourished.

It isn't just babies who thrive when given loving attention.

As part of his research, you will remember, Dr. John Gottman had couples spend a whole day in an apartment just "hanging out," watching TV, reading a book or the paper, eating meals—whatever they would normally do on a day off.

Watching the videotapes he had made after he knew which couples ended up divorced years later and which ended up happy together, Gottman noticed something the happy couples did around 80% of the time that the couples who got divorced did only about 30% of the time. What the couples were doing differently was often so subtle that it was easy to miss, but this difference had a huge impact on whether or not the marriages survived and flourished.

Gottman called the pattern "turning toward bids."

One of the partners would make what Gottman called a "bid" for attention. Perhaps she would say, "These eggs you cooked are really good." Perhaps he would read aloud a passage from the book he was immersed in. Perhaps she would say, as she looked out the window at the nearby lake, "What a pretty boat!"

What was critical is what the other partner did next.

Perhaps he or she would respond, "Oh" or "Uh huh." Just that! Just acknowledging that s/he had heard what the partner said. Of course, s/he could respond with more enthusiasm or interest: "Glad you like the eggs." Wow, that's an interesting idea." "What kind of boat?"

Either way, Gottman called that response "turning toward" the bid. That's what the couples did whose marriages lasted and became better with the passing years.

How else could the partner respond? By doing nothing, not showing in any way that they had heard what the partner said. Gottman called this "turning away" from the bid.

Or by saying something like, "Can't you see I'm busy?" Or, "I'm TRYING to do this CROSSWORD puzzle!" Gottman called this "turning against" the bid.

Either way, turning away or turning against, that was what the couples who got divorced did 2/3 of the time.

Notice, even the couples who got divorced turned toward their partners' bids 1/3 of the time. And the couples whose marriages lasted and got better didn't turn toward EVERY bid. But they turned toward most of them, and *the ones who got divorced didn't*.

You're important to me

When we're dating, of course, we pay a lot of attention to the person we're dating. We make it clear by what we say and by small gifts that we bring and by calling or texting them that we are thinking about them. We express in many ways that they and the relationship are special to us. We make it known that this relationship and this person are important to us.

And when we do, the person usually responds with pleasure. S/he turns toward our bid. Probably not just 80%, but close to 100% of the time!

And at that stage, our relationships flourish.

How can you pay attention to your mate now?

For starters, you can turn toward your partner's bids. When your partner says, "I heard something interesting today," you can respond with interest (instead of ignoring the comment or saying, "Hey, I'm trying to check my email!"). "With interest" means turning away from the screen and giving your partner your full attention when you say, "Tell me about it!"

If your partner is reading and says, "Amazing," you'll say, "What's amazing?" When your partner is looking out the window or walking with you and says, "That's beautiful," you'll find out what's beautiful and if it's still visible, share your own response.

If your partner says, "I just read a fascinating article. The author thinks he's made a connection between the quantum field and special and general relativity! He has the idea that..." the way my wife Kari just did as I was getting my breakfast (she did, really!), and if you are in the middle of something else (like me thinking about what I was about to write in this chapter!), you can still turn toward the bid by interrupting and saying something like, "Hey Hon, that sounds cool and I really want to hear about it, but I can't take it in right now. I'm thinking about something else. Could you tell me about it later?"

What can you do to strengthen your relationship besides turn toward your partner's bids?

A is for Affection

Part of what feels so good when you're dating is suddenly having someone who is acting affectionate toward you. Whether with a smile when you enter the room, a hug or a kiss, or by leaving a note where you will find it, the person is continually finding ways to express affection that will touch you and brighten your day.

All these expressions of affection are ways of saying, "I like you. I feel good about you." And also, "I was thinking about you." They're ways of paying attention to you.

"I was thinking about you."

One of Kari's favorite songs is "I just called to say I love you." Once in awhile, I'll call and sing her that line. She will laugh with pleasure, knowing I was thinking about her.

Other times I'll see something that reminds me of her, and I'll text her about it or snap a picture with my phone and text the photo to her.

Exactly the kinds of things we did when we were dating.

Some people tell their partners about things they saw people doing that they think their partner would like to hear about, or bring home surprise gifts, or tell their partner jokes or funny stories they heard.

What did you do when *you* were dating?

"But I don't THINK of doing things like that!"

That's exactly the point. The reason so many relationships sink into The Blahs is that we get busy thinking about all sorts of other things and STOP thinking about our mates.

This is a habit we can change. But it takes attention and some effort to change it.

Here's one way to do it: Put a small sign with your partner's name on it on your desk or someplace you will see it. Then when you notice the sign, think of a way to reach out to your partner, and if at all possible, DO it. (Move the sign every week or so, or you will stop noticing it!)

Here's another: set an alarm to go off sometime during the morning, and another one to go off sometime during the afternoon. When the alarms go off, take just a moment to think of your partner and either reach out right then or plan a way to reach out later. Think of something you've heard or seen that they would enjoy or be interested in, etc.

Here's one more: When you DO spontaneously think of a way to reach out to your partner, ACT on it.

To increase your repertoire of ways to give attention to your mate and your relationship, you can do the exercise called "Thinking of You" at www.drkonline.com/dymbonus.

OK, "A" is for *Appreciation*, and for giving your partner and your relationship the *Attention* that brings them to life. (These are also a good way to express your *Affection!*) What about "B?"

Before we explore B, we need to understand a myth that can undermine everything we're doing together. When people believe this myth, the impact is so destructive—and so insidious—that I think about it as *"The Hidden Myth that Kills Relationships."*

CHAPTER EIGHT

How to Beat the Hidden Myth That Kills Relationships

There is a myth that kills thousands of relationships before they even start and many more relationships after that. This myth is a major cause of The Blah's.

The myth is driven deep into our psyches by stories we hear as children, by books, movies, TV, by the covers of the tabloid newspapers and magazines we see at the checkout counter at the grocery store. It's all around us.

Some of us believe that it's not a myth, but the truth. More of us would say we don't really believe it, but at some level nearly all of us do. Most of us aren't even aware that we think this way. But it shapes our actions and kills our relationships whether we know that we believe it or not.

This myth takes many forms, but at the core it is a deceptively simple idea.

I call it *"The Myth of the Soul Mate."*

A magic moment

According to the myth, each of us has a soul mate out there somewhere, waiting for us. Someday, somewhere, if we're incredibly lucky, we will find each other. We will gaze into each other's eyes or we will feel a touch, and in that magic moment, we will know. We will feel a connection like no other, and our lives will never be the same.

Until we meet our soul mate, it's as if we are living in a black-and-white movie—perhaps even a silent movie. When two soul mates find each other the movie shifts to color and beautiful music swells.

Beyond words

When we and our soul mate find each other, a lifetime of yearning is suddenly fulfilled. All our unmet needs are satisfied. Our days are filled with joy, and our nights—well our nights are simply indescribable!

Finding our soul mate, it almost goes without saying, is the real key to living happily ever after.

What damage can this do?

"This is a nice fantasy," you may be thinking. "If it's true, of course, it means that a few lucky people who manage to find their soul mates have something wonderful to look forward to. But whether it's true or not, what damage can it do to believe it?"

I believe the damage is incalculable.

Is this "the One?"

Many people would scoff at the idea that somewhere their soul mates are waiting for them. But how many times have you heard someone say, "I'm looking for Mr. Right," or "You know, I think this person I just made met may be "the One?"

However they would express it, or even if they would never put it into words, even to themselves, how many people do you suppose are hoping or dreaming in their heart of hearts that the perfect person for them is out there—and that they will find each other and have the perfect relationship that being with that perfect person will make possible?

There's only one problem. *This innocent hope poisons every relationship it touches!*

The search

First, the Myth of the Soul Mate (or "the One") can undermine or damage every casual contact.

If we're on the hunt, each time we meet a new person who seems in any way attractive we shift into evaluation mode. Instead of simply enjoying each new acquaintanceship for whatever it has to offer, we add the freight of going through a mental checklist. "Smile? Check. Body type? Check. Sense of humor? Check. Makes my heart flutter and my knees grow weak? Check…"

It's wired into our genes, of course, to be looking for a mate. But this is far more restrictive: we are not looking for *A* mate, we're looking for *THE* mate.

"No, I don't think so. NEXT?"

The result? Our list is likely to be so restrictive that we weed out many many people with whom we could have had a perfectly wonderful relationship, or even a wonderful marriage.

This is the first way the Myth of the Soul Mate kills relationships. But the damage has just begun.

Suppose we find someone who's truly wonderful and we fall in love. We decide to get married. The Myth of the Soul Mate continues to distort our perception and our feelings. It's likely to poison even our wedding day!

Am I settling?

No matter how wonderful the person we're marrying is, there will be at least some items on our list that this person doesn't quite meet. This will leave us with the nagging fear that by marrying this person, we are making the biggest mistake of our lives: We are missing out on the phenomenal relationship we might have had—could have had—*would* have had if we had waited to meet our soul mate.

This may even limit the depth of the commitment we are actually making on our wedding day. At a level so deep we may not even be aware of it, we are really promising that we'll stay with this marriage "till death do us part–*unless my soul mate shows up!*"

This can lay the groundwork for an affair later that will blindside our mate and even us.

So we enter the marriage in a state of doubt and incomplete commitment. But the poison continues to work.

"My soul mate would never do that!"

Because the myth IS a myth—even someone who is 99% perfect for us is not 100% perfect— sooner or later (and probably sooner!) our new mate will do something that clearly isn't "right."

Maybe he leaves his underwear on the floor of the bedroom, or belches or passes gas in a way that she finds really embarrassing.

Maybe she takes forever to get ready for a party—or makes a cutting remark at the party about an idea he expressed.

Whatever it is, the impact goes far beyond minor annoyance. It can be the beginning of the end. Because both people realize immediately: *"My soul mate would never do something like that."*

When added to at first dozens and then hundreds and then thousands of similar experiences, it leads to a single inescapable conclusion:

"I made a mistake! This isn't the One. *I married the wrong person!!*"

NOW what?

Here's what is most devastating about believing that we have chosen poorly: According to the myth of the Soul Mate, we are left with only two options. We can admit we made a mistake, end the relationship, and return to the search for our soul mate. Or we can settle for a relationship we know isn't right and do what we can to make the best of it.

Work on the relationship? What for?

When it becomes apparent that our relationship is troubled, someone may suggest that we go to a counselor or therapist or read a book or attend a workshop and work on the relationship to try to make it better.

We may resist this approach, trying to deny the Awful Truth about not being with our soul mate, saying, "Oh, it isn't really that bad."

Or we may try to make things better, but our heart won't really be in it. Because we know that no matter how hard we work, no matter what we do to try to make this relationship better, we can't solve our fundamental problem. No matter how much better things get, if we stay with this person we are doomed to live in a relationship that is far from what we really want. Because the fundamental problem is that we are with the wrong person.

We may hope that somehow counseling or therapy or an act of God will fix our mate and turn this defective person into our soul mate. But we don't really believe it. So if we do work on our relationship, we do it half-heartedly. And the results show it.

I know this sounds pretty bleak. Unfortunately, for too many people it's reality. Variations on this scenario cause untold misery for couples all over the world. Fortunately, I have good news.

It just isn't true!

The reason I'm talking about this is that as long as you think at some level that there is a "right person" for you, you are virtually certain to have relationships that are far from what they could be.

And you are virtually certain not to get everything you could out of taking my courses or reading my books or working with me or anyone else in person!

Because you will be looking in the wrong place to discover what you can do to have a truly wonderful relationship.

You will think the right things to do are

#1 to be on the lookout for the right person, and

#2 to constantly evaluate whether you are with the right person.

You won't realize the kernel of truth in the myth of the Soul Mate and what you can do to help that kernel blossom into a truly satisfying relationship—with almost anyone!

The kernel of truth

The fact is, the kind of wonderful, joyous, deeply satisfying relationship promised by the myth of the soul mate does exist. It *is* available to you.

It's what we are built for. It's the kind of relationship we are designed to have.

But not just with one person—your soul mate—"Mr. Right" or "Ms. Right"—"the One."

This is the kind of relationship we are designed to have with *anyone* when we open fully to each other.

It's the kind of relationship we glimpse from time to time with many people, and that we experience for a bit longer when we fall in love.

It's the kind of relationship we *never* feel when we are closed off—contracted out of fear or lost in a judgmental, evaluative attitude.

So, ironically, the more we are evaluating every moment of every human contact to determine whether this person is our soul mate or "the right person for me" or "the One," the less we are likely to experience what we are looking for.

The bottom line

So here's the point: the more you can do whatever it takes to open up to your partner and encourage your partner to open up to you, the more you will experience the kind of relationship you have always wanted.

Every chapter in every book I've written, every principle I teach, every tool in my toolkit—everything we do if you decide to meet with me in person or via Skype—is designed to help you do exactly that. But in many ways reading this chapter may be the most important single thing you can do if it helps you to realize that the notion of "the right person for me" is a myth. That you can have a "soul mate" relationship with just about anyone—almost certainly including the person you're in a relationship with right now.

I say "almost certainly" to remind you to use your common sense. Improving a truly destructive relationship is beyond the scope of any book. If your partner is so abusive psychologically

> *or physically that you fear for your sanity or your physical safety, please go online and Google "abuse hotline" to find someone with whom you can discuss your situation and make a plan to keep yourself—and your children if children are involved—safe. Do it now!*
>
> *Don't worry—if your partner is destructive or abusive in these ways, you may not want to admit it, but you know it! If not, you can safely disregard this message.*

So if you find yourself slipping into old habitual thinking like, "Oh my gosh, I wonder if I'm with the wrong person," just remember *"Oh wait a minute—there's no such thing as 'the right person for me!' That's just that silly myth."* And let the thoughts go.

Then just go back to using the other ideas this book has sparked in you to build the relationship of your dreams with the person you're sharing your life with right now!

Now then: we've talked about A: Attention, Appreciation, and Affection. What about B?

CHAPTER NINE

B Is for "Break the Routine"

If you think about it, one of the biggest contributors to The Blahs is that when you are dating, being together is new and fresh—a break in your daily routine. Each date is a unique event. You never know what is going to happen next.

After you've been together for a while, being together *is* the routine. A predictable routine can feel good at first. It gives you a feeling of security, something you can count on in a world that is too often chaotic. But when something starts happening over and over and over and over again, how does it start to feel? Often, BORRRING!

Enter "The Blahs."

Adding "juice" to a relationship

A great way to rescue your relationship from boredom and The Blahs is to arrange *breaks* from the routine.

> *My wife Kari likes to drink organic fruit and vegetable juices.*
>
> *It actually takes quite a bit of time and effort to chop all the fruit and vegetables, make the juices, and clean up.*
>
> *Every so often out of the blue I'll say, "Hey sweetheart, would you like me to make you a juice?" She always melts and with a big smile says, "That would be WONDERFUL!"*

Notice, this actually wouldn't be as impactful if I did it every day. And that's a good thing, because I wouldn't WANT to do it every day!

But once in a while, it's a nice break in my routine AND a great break in Kari's routine.

One of my chores that DOES happen every day is that I wash the dishes.

Every so often, out of the blue, Kari will say, "Don't bother with the dishes tonight, honey. I'll take care of them."

I feel wonderful! I feel like a kid playing Monopoly, and I just got a "Get out of jail free!" card!

These kinds of surprise offers carry lot of impact—a lot of refreshment for our relationship, for just a little extra thought and effort.

"I'm coming over."

When you were dating, think what a nice surprise it was when your partner called to say, "Are you free? I'd like to come over."

You can do the same thing with your mate.

You can call and suggest meeting for lunch. Or, in the middle of the afternoon. (THAT can get downright exciting!)

Or you can suggest meeting at a park after work to take a walk.

Or to add a little mystery, suggest meeting at a certain intersection or address—and have in mind a nearby restaurant or movie or museum or gallery to take your mate to.

Remember we talked about paying attention to your partner when you part or get back together? Here's a way to break the routine that will add a lot of impact to a moment like that.

How to supercharge your greeting

Remember what it was like the first time you held hands with someone?

> *I remember the first time I held hands with a girl. My mom was driving us to a high school dance and we were sitting together in the back seat of the car. Our hands touched. I felt an almost overpowering desire to take her hand in mine, so I did. The feeling was electric! After that, every time my mom drove us somewhere we held hands in the back of the car. We never did anything more overtly sexual—we didn't even kiss until weeks later!—but I was in heaven each time we held hands.*

When I heard the Beatles' song *"I Want to Hold Your Hand,"* I realized I wasn't alone.

Why is holding hands so powerful?

A boost from oxytocin

Here's a fascinating fact: When you make skin contact with another person for just 6 seconds, your body starts to secrete a hormone called oxytocin. Oxytocin is the "bonding" hormone—it helps mothers bond with their babies. But it also predisposes *any* two people to feel closer. It's not about sex. It's about closeness and being connected.

This, by the way, is one of the reasons for a phenomenon that puzzles many women: how come after a fight, a man often wants to have sex? Most women need to feel close before they will want to make love. So they wonder, "How can he want to make love when we're still mad at each other or feeling distant?"

It's because for most men it's the other way around: They feel close AFTER sex. A big reason is the oxytocin in their systems generated by the skin contact they've just shared with their partner.

In any case, a powerful—and enjoyable!—way to increase your focus on each other when you get back together after you've been apart is with some physical contact.

A hug is good, but skin contact is even better—as long as it lasts at least six seconds.

Which leads to one of the most powerful suggestions from Dr. John Gottman.

The kiss that can save your marriage

When he lectures on his findings about what makes marriages last, Dr. Gottman will frequently stop and begin counting 1... 2... 3... 4... 5... 6... "That was six seconds," he'll say. "That seems like a long time. But that's how long a kiss should last if you want to really get your partner's attention!"

He's talking, of course, about oxytocin.

So if you want to supercharge The Marriage Saver, combine greeting each other with a hug and a six-second kiss. Whether you include the kiss every time is up to you. Probably it will have more impact if you *don't*. Just do it once in awhile to add spice—to break the routine.

And remember, not just a quick peck. Six full seconds!

This is how you keep your relationship fresh.

The point is to break out of your blah routine—to do or suggest something your mate doesn't expect, but something you think your mate will like.

> *For a list of ways you can break out of your blah routine, get "Breaking Out of the Routine" to jump start your own creativity at* www.drkonline.com/dymbonus.

It's easy to overlook how dangerous a boring routine can be to your relationship but once you become aware, it's also pretty easy to fix.

There is another danger—one that probably kills more relationships than anything else except maybe the Myth of the Soul Mate (see the chapter on *"How to Beat the Hidden Myth that Kills Relationships"*). This danger is more obvious. But it can also be even harder to deal with. It's a danger that blindsides most of us over and over again. And dealing with it well requires a different kind of break…

CHAPTER TEN

Where Did THAT Come From?

OK, so we are consciously making a point of appreciating our mate's good qualities and all the thing they do—even the little things—to make our life easier and nicer.

We're intentionally building positive sentiment override, because we know that the more we look for positives about our mate and our relationship, the more we will see.

But what about the negatives? What about our mate's *bad* qualities, the things we DON'T appreciate?

And what about the times when it's hard to find anything to appreciate?

Does this mean we have to lie to ourselves, to pretend our partners never do anything negative?

No, lying to ourselves is never a good idea. On the other hand, you will remember that the couples who benefitted from positive sentiment override didn't make as big a deal of the negatives. In fact, they often didn't notice them. They had a habit of doing what nearly all of us do when we are dating.

When we are dating, we give the person we're dating the benefit of the doubt. We cut them some slack.

And we are wise to do this. Here's why:

There is something puzzling that occurs in all human relationships—even while we're dating. You've probably noticed it yourself. If so, you've probably wondered what was going on.

Where did s/he go?

We're going happily along and then suddenly, often without warning, the wonderful person we're dating disappears and is replaced by someone we don't recognize—a much less attractive, sometimes even scary version of himself or herself. It's like Robert Louis Stevenson's story of Dr. Jekyll and Mr. Hyde.

You've probably heard at least the bare bones of the story.

> *The main character in the story is Dr. Jekyll. Dr. Jekyll is friendly, sociable, and virtuous. But sometimes, without warning, Dr. Jekyll is transformed into someone quite different: the brutish, even dangerous Mr. Hyde.*

We are all Dr. Jekyll and Mr. Hyde!

Unfortunately, all of us sometimes momentarily undergo a similar transformation—maybe not as extreme as the shift from Dr. Jekyll to Mr. Hyde, but very real and disconcerting nonetheless. This can be confusing not only to others but even to ourselves.

We get in an argument and suddenly we find that we are saying things and doing things—hurtful things—that seem completely out of character. We're suddenly shouting at our partner, or throwing things, or even becoming physically violent.

Or we're in a fog, unable to think straight. Or the situation suddenly feels intolerable. We feel, "I can't stand this any more" and we suddenly have to get away. Right in the middle of a conversation we leave—and maybe we slam the door as we go out. And our partner wonders, "Where did THAT come from?"

Amygdala hijack!

Where it came from is a small structure in our brain called the amygdala. We actually have two of them—little almond-shaped structures about an inch inside our temples. Ironically, our amygdalas are there to keep us safe, but they can get us in a lot of trouble! Here's why.

Physiologically, we actually almost have three brains, not one. Inside our heads are three fairly distinct layers of neurons with three separate functions.

At the center of our brain are a set of structures that regulate primitive behaviors like keeping our balance and finding food and procreation, territorial behavior and dominance and submission. You may have heard this set of structures talked about as the "reptilian" brain, because these structures are very similar to the whole brain of a snake or frog or salamander. This part of our brain operates mainly on the basis of survival instinct and habit.

Have you ever been driving and discovered that you had passed your exit a few miles back, or noticed to your dismay that you were on your way to work even though it was your day off? That's the reptilian brain in action. When you're on automatic, acting without thinking, it's usually the reptilian brain driving your behavior.

Around the reptilian brain structures is a layer that is quite different. This layer has to do with emotion, hate and love, bonding. Reptiles don't have much in the way of emotions. That's why a frog doesn't make a very good pet. Kittens and puppies have more of this second brain layer. Some researchers call this the "mammalian" brain.

But puppies and kittens have a very limited ability to think. That's the job of the third brain layer, the neocortex. And there's a region of the neocortex—right behind our high foreheads—called the prefrontal cortex that makes possible most of our distinctly human capacities. It's because of our prefrontal cortex that we can imagine the future and make plans, empathize with others, and be aware of and regulate our own behavior.

And right between the prefrontal cortex and the emotional brain sits the amygdala.

> *Imagine that you are walking across a busy street, lost in thought, and a huge bus is bearing down on you. Out of the corner of your eye, you notice the bus.*
>
> *What you would NOT want to do is spend several minutes thinking up a 45-step plan you could use to get to safety.*
>
> *You wouldn't want to spend a while imagining what the results will be like if the bus hits you.*
>
> *You wouldn't want to be empathizing with the bus driver, thinking about how upset he will be if he runs over you.*
>
> *In other words, you DON'T want your prefrontal cortex to be active.*
>
> *Fortunately, your amygdala is on the job.*
>
> *Your amygdala sends a quick DANGER! message to your prefrontal cortex AND THEN SHUTS IT DOWN! Your prefrontal cortex doesn't go completely off-line, but most of the blood and the source of most activity shifts to your emotional and habit brains. And you're OUT OF THERE! Without even knowing quite what happened, you're standing on the sidewalk, watching the bus go past.*

What do we call that reaction?

Most people call it the "fight or flight" reaction, because our amygdalas originally dealt with threats like saber-tooth tigers, not buses, so fighting or fleeing—or freezing, so a predator won't notice us—is what this reaction is wired in to help us do.

But Daniel Goleman, in his groundbreaking book *Emotional Intelligence,* dubbed it an "emotional hijack." I call it an *amygdala hijack,* because what's really happening is that *the amygdala is hijacking your brain—taking your higher thought processes offline and putting your emotional and habit brains in charge.*

And while that can save your life if a bus is bearing down on you, it can also be hazardous to your health. Or someone else's.

It can even get somebody killed!

Daniel Goleman describes a tragic example:

> *"Fourteen-Year-old Matilda Crabtree was just playing a practical joke on her father: she jumped out of a closet and yelled "Boo!" when her parents came home at 1 a.m.*
>
> *But Bobby Crabtree and his wife thought Matilda was staying with friends that night. Hearing noises as he entered the house, Crabtree reached for his .357 caliber pistol and went into Matilda's bedroom to investigate. When his daughter jumped from the closet, Crabtree shot her in the neck. Matilda Crabtree died twelve hours later.* (Emotional Intelligence, New York: Bantam Books, 1995, p.4)

Here's the problem: The amygdala is very fast. That can be good if you're in danger. But it's also very stupid. It goes into action immediately when we feel threatened and powerless: when our amygdala senses danger. But our amygdala identifies anything *resembling* danger as "DANGER"—and that can be very bad.

The birth of Mr./Ms. Hyde

This is where Mr. Hyde or Ms. Hyde comes from. Your amygdala senses something that looks like danger and BANG! It shuts down your prefrontal cortex and amps up your emotions and your sense of urgency—generating the almost overwhelming feeling that something has to be *done*—RIGHT NOW! And the "something" is not usually pretty.

That's often when you say the things you later wish you hadn't said, or do the things you wish you hadn't done.

That is when people quit perfectly good jobs, or walk out on perfectly good marriages. Or do things that damage those marriages beyond repair. Or even kill people they love.

How can you keep this from happening in YOUR relationships?

First you have to recognize that an amygdala hijack is in progress. You have to know you're being hijacked—or your partner is!

How to recognize an amygdala hijack

Fortunately, the signals are not subtle. You can easily learn to recognize them.

"I'm upset!"

The first clue that you're being hijacked is often your emotions. If you feel angry or scared—or numb—you're probably being hijacked. (Even the term "upset" points to the problem: you are emotionally off balance. You're "unbalanced.")

You may notice body sensations like sweaty palms or tension in your gut or your jaw. You may feel your hands starting to form fists. Or you may notice your heart beating fast or your breathing becoming rapid and shallow or that you are holding your breath.

Or the first signs you notice may be changes in your thinking.

"I can't think straight."

In the middle of an amygdala hijack, remember, your prefrontal cortex largely shuts down. That means it gets harder for you to think clearly.

Your psychological field narrows. You may find it hard to understand what people are saying. You may start thinking the same thoughts—maybe fearful or angry thoughts—over and over. Your thoughts may be racing. Or you may feel like your brain has frozen, and you can hardly think at all.

"Things really look BAD!"

One of the most insidious effects of an amygdala hijack is also one of the hardest to recognize... until you know what to look for.

It's as if a cloud has covered the sun—or your whole life!

To understand what happens, think about what occurs when you are out driving and you start to get hungry.

> *You may not even be consciously aware of being hungry at first, but suddenly you start noticing restaurants.*
>
> *You may be passing dozens of stores, but they don't register. As far as you're concerned, it's as if they weren't there. But every restaurant you pass starts showing up in living color.*

This happens automatically, as soon as you need food. THEN you start to notice, "Hey—I'm getting hungry!"

> *Remember the last time you were in the market for a new car or a new electronic gadget? Suddenly the roads were full of cars like that, or you saw those gadgets and ads for them everywhere you went. You didn't try to. It just happened.*

This is how our perceptual system works: whatever is related to a need we have comes into the foreground. Everything else recedes into the background.

Because your amygdala is primed to look for danger—and what your brain is primed to see, you see more of—when the amygdala is active nearly everything you see looks bad, even dangerous.

Your partner looks like a jerk. Your relationship looks like a big mistake with serious problems. Even your life starts to look bad—ruined by this awful relationship!

We don't know that our perceptions are skewed and distorted. In the middle of a hijack, we can't see all the good things about our mate, our relationship, our life. Or if we remember them at all, it's as if they don't count (like all those stores that simply aren't relevant when we're on a quest for food).

Once you know to look for it, this distorted perception can be a clear indicator that you are in an amygdala hijack.

But watch out! All the negative things you are seeing about your partner and your relationship and your life will still look just as real and just as hopeless even if you know your perception must be off, just as knowing you are looking in a fun-house mirror doesn't change the weird wiggly way your body and everything around you looks.

But at least once you notice how everything has suddenly gone negative you are less likely to get carried away by what I call "dysfunctional urgency."

"I've got to do something NOW!"

What causes most of the damage during an amygdala hijack is also one of the clearest indicators that a hijack is in progress: an almost irresistible impulse to do or say something —immediately!

You suddenly find it hard to let someone finish her sentence without telling her she's wrong: That's *not* what happened, that's not what you did at all. That's not what you *meant!* You may feel like hitting somebody. Or like running out of the room.

Your distorted perception that your relationship has Big Problems may generate the feeling that you've GOT to sort this out—you've got to get to the bottom of it and get it solved—NOW.

Unfortunately, now is probably the *worst* time to try to sort something out, because at the moment you've got the intelligence of celery. Remember, most of your real intelligence—your ability to empathize and use your imagination and make fine distinctions—is unavailable because your prefrontal cortex is mostly offline.

For an exercise that can help you identify the signals to look for that will tell you when you are in the middle of an amygdala hijack and help you install a "Tripwire" that will automatically warn you so you don't do something stupid while part of your brain is off line, go to www.drkonline.com/dymbonus *and download the "I'm Being Hijacked!" Technique. (This exercise is well worth doing. It can literally change the course of your life!)*

So: you're feeling upset, you can't think straight, your partner looks like a jerk, your relationship looks like a disaster, and your life is a mess—and you feel like you've got to do something about it all NOW. You're clearly in the middle of an amygdala hijack.

You *know* it, but what can you *do* about it?

CHAPTER ELEVEN

"Our equipment isn't working right"

The critical 1/10 of a second

One of the most important pieces of research I read recently noted that about 1/10 of a second before our amygdala hijacks our brain, it sends a signal to our frontal lobes saying "Danger!"

This is important because if you recognize that signal, you have an opportunity to realize what is about to happen. 1/10 of a second isn't long, but it's long enough to tell your amygdala to cool it.

It would have been long enough for Bobby Crabtree to check out the situation before pulling the trigger and shooting his daughter Matilda.

You yourself have almost certainly experienced that 1/10 of a second.

Remember a time when you were in an "intense discussion" (all right, an argument!) with someone dear to you. You said the kind of thing you always say, and the other person said what they always say. You responded the way you always do, and they responded back the way they always do. As your tempers got shorter and shorter and emotion rose higher and higher, you got to the point where you were just about to say something—and you KNEW that if you said it things would not go well.

Then you said it anyway, and things fell apart. Or you didn't.

Either way, it's that instant I'm talking about: when you *knew* it wouldn't be good to say it. Then you were awash in dysfunctional urgency and it was almost—but *not quite*—impossible to hold back from saying it.

That 1/10 of a second of awareness is important, because it means that each time another escalation is about to happen, we have a brief window of opportunity to choose a different path.

But what different path can we take?

When you recognize that you're in the middle of an amygdala hijack—or about to be hijacked—what can you *do*?

"Our equipment isn't working right"

When Dr. Gottman was observing couples in his lab, he noticed an interesting correlation.

From time to time, one or both partners would have a sudden rise in heart rate. Their hearts would start beating much faster than usual.

And at the same time, their conversation would degenerate. It suddenly seemed to be harder for them to understand each other. They couldn't resolve the simplest issues.

Gottman decided to try an experiment. The next time a couple's heart rates went way up, he came out from behind his one-way mirror and told hem, "Our equipment isn't working quite right. Could you please take a break in your conversation for a few minutes? You can just read these magazines quietly."

Then he went back behind his one-way mirror and waited until their heart rates had dropped back to normal.

When he then told the couple, "OK, you can continue now," Gottman was astonished by what he saw. He described the result in a talk I heard him give:

"It was as if they had gotten a brain transplant! Suddenly they were discussing rationally and calmly what they had hardly been able to talk about at all a few minutes before. They were able to understand each other. . . It was as if they were two different people."

When we're in the middle of an amygdala hijack, it's as if *our* equipment—our *brain*—isn't working right.

Fortunately, *an amygdala hijack is self-limiting.* At some point your amygdala calms down and you get your intelligence back. Unfortunately, by the time that happens you may already have said things you wish you hadn't and burned bridges that are hard to rebuild.

So *your first priority as soon as you realize an amygdala hijack is in progress is to limit the damage.*

This can be harder than you would think it should be. The reason is the almost irresistible momentum toward MAD.

Don't get MAD!

During the cold war, both the United States and the Soviet Union had so many nuclear weapons that there was the very real possibility that most of civilization would be destroyed in a single exchange.

Unbelievably, this was exactly the point of the strategy both sides had adopted. The danger was created intentionally.

Each side trusted the other so little that the only way they felt they could be certain of not being attacked was to make sure the other side knew that in case of attack they would be obliterated too. The doctrine was called Mutually Assured Destruction—MAD.

Despite an amazing number of near misses, we have avoided that cataclysm so far. But closer to home, many couples have fights—sometimes regularly—that escalate to the point where there is a real danger that the relationship will not survive—that someone will finally say "No more of this" and file for divorce. Or that someone will get seriously injured or killed.

Why does this escalation so often take place? One reason is our mirror neurons.

Our mirror neurons may do us in

Fairly recently, researchers have discovered a remarkable source of empathy. Not only can we figure out what someone is feeling by thinking about it. We can also literally feel what they are feeling.

It turns out that we have certain brain cells—researchers have dubbed them "mirror neurons"—that fire when we become aware that someone is having a certain feeling. Then they give us the same kind of experience that person is having. Say we see someone stub his toe. We may actually get a momentary feeling of our own toe hurting!

Well, what if our mate is feeling threatened and powerless—in the middle of an amygdala hijack? (Who knows why? It doesn't matter—our mate's amygdala may have been triggered by something completely innocent that we did. In any case, s/he's feeling threatened and powerless, and beginning to act like Mr. Hyde.)

Our mirror neurons are likely to trigger a similar set of feelings in us. So even if we were feeling fine, out of the blue we suddenly start feeling threatened and powerless too!

In addition, when Mr. Hyde appears that IS a threat—the threat of losing our connection with our mate. And if we quickly discover that we can't get through to our mate to straighten things out, we begin to feel even more threatened and powerless. Which triggers *our* amygdala, and suddenly we are *both* getting hijacked. All at once we don't have the intelligence to respond calmly and rationally to whatever our partner is saying to us.

So we respond unwisely, by saying or doing something that further triggers our partner. And we're off to the races.

And it's very hard to STOP.

"I've got to say just one more thing!"

What does most of the damage during an amygdala hijack isn't usually the first thing or two you say or do. Shooting somebody by mistake is, fortunately, pretty rare.

What does the serious damage is the third or sixth or tenth thing, after the almost inevitable escalation. The more threatened and powerless we each feel, the more we feel dysfunctional urgency—that we HAVE to do something RIGHT NOW to protect ourself or get through to our partner.

Our partner experiences whatever we do as an attack and defends against it, or a wall that they try to smash their way through to reconnect with us, which of course doesn't work. Each back-and-forth interchange drives us farther apart. So we feel *more* threatened, more desperate, and less able to do anything wise even as we feel more urgently that we HAVE to do SOMETHING.

The only way to limit the damage is to stop the escalation—as soon as possible. And the only way to do that is to *bite your tongue and NOT SAY the next thing you urgently want to say*.

This is the hard part. It's still what gets Kari and me off track sometimes, even though we know all about amygdala hijacks. It's *so tempting* to say "just one more thing." But it never works. It always makes things worse.

What works when your "equipment isn't working right" is to do what Dr. Gottman did when he noticed the signs that his couples were getting hijacked: *Stop the action and take a break.*

That's how you can give *yourselves* a brain transplant!

The amygdala shift: "Let's stop here and talk later."

After lots of practice, Kari and I have learned that instead of saying the "just one more thing" that we're dying to say, the only thing that will work out well is to say something like, "We're not getting anywhere. Let's stop here for now!" or words to that effect.

And—equally hard—we've learned to accept that when the other person says it, we really do need to stop right there and just say "OK" instead of replying with the "just one more thing" *we* were on the verge of saying.

I call this the *amygdala shift:* shifting from being engaged with the argument or interaction that is going downhill to limiting the damage by taking a break.

So "B" is also *"When you notice you're in an amygdala hijack... Bite your tongue and take a Break!"*

How to blow it

Besides saying "just one more thing," there are a couple of ways to move toward taking a break that will NOT work.

"YOU are being impossible!"

First, anything you say about what is going on has to be completely neutral, without an ounce of blame—even if at the moment you are completely convinced it's all your partner's fault.

"I'm not going to talk to you until you calm down" or "If you're going to be this way about it, there's nothing more to say!" won't cut it.

The message needs to be simply "WE are off the tracks and WE need to take a break to get our bearings back." No implication whatever about whose fault it is or how innocent you are. Otherwise the other person will feel they have to defend themselves and the escalation will begin again.

Just walking out isn't taking a break, it's flight!

One of the clearest patterns Dr. Gottman noticed that predicts divorce is what he calls "stonewalling." When one person—typically the woman—attacks and criticizes and complains, the other—typically the man—sits with arms folded, not saying anything, often not looking at his partner, apparently unaffected, When Dr. Gottman checked, he discovered that someone stonewalling is anything but unaffected. In fact, his heart rate is climbing through the roof. He is deep in an amygdala hijack, but he's trying to suppress it: To try to avoid having things escalate, he is not responding at all. When Gottman interviewed people who were stonewalling, he found that they were trying to keep things from getting worse by not saying all the angry things they were thinking.

Unfortunately, while not expressing his anger may have been a good idea, this approach simply makes his partner feel more threatened and powerless: there is no way she can get through to him. So the more he does this, the more she escalates her attempts to reach him.

> *Kari and I used to get into a similar pattern: We would get into an escalation and Kari would walk out of the room. Her instinct was right—we had to stop the action to get our bearings back.*
>
> *But when she left, I got even more triggered. I felt (maybe remembering my mother leaving my dad) like our connection was breaking and I was in danger of losing her forever. So I would follow her into the next room, and the escalation would continue. (This is a pattern that frequently leads to domestic violence, although we fortunately never escalated that far.)*

What we learned to do—and what *you* need to do—is not just leave the scene. (Especially, much as you may feel like doing it, don't storm out and slam the door!) Instead, *let your partner know that you want to take a break BUT THAT YOU ARE COMING BACK.*

"I'm starting to lose it, Hon. I need to take a walk and calm down. Could we continue this in 20 minutes or so?"

The hardest part of this whole process is shifting from playing your part in an escalation to stopping the action GRACEFULLY so you can take a break. For a technique that can help you develop a habit that will make this a good deal easier, you can go now to www.drkonline.com/dymbonus and download "The Amygdala Shift."

So to limit the dangerous escalation and get your intelligence back, you need to bite your tongue and take a break.

But what do you do during the break?

CHAPTER TWELVE

Getting Your Intelligence Back

OK, you've disentangled yourself from a situation involving an amygdala hijack. Instead of continuing to escalate, you're taking a break. What can you do during the break to get your intelligence back as quickly as possible? Like this...

Breathe!

The first thing you can do is take a few long, slow deep breaths—with a longer exhale than inhale. If you breathe in deeply, hold your breath for a moment, and then breathe out even longer than you breathed in, you will soon find yourself calming down.

This works because when you are in the midst of an amygdala hijack, you ordinarily breathe rapidly, shallowly, or not at all—you hold your breath. The only time you normally breathe slowly and deeply is when your feel safe and things are fine.

So by breathing this way you can communicate with your own nervous system that "Appearances to the contrary notwithstanding, I'm safe and things are fine!" Then your amygdala will relax and stand down.

Move!

We all have habitual ways of holding our bodies that go with certain feeling states. One of the most powerful ways to change how we feel is to move: to stand up and stretch, to dance, to go for a walk. Moving rhythmically as you do when you walk also leads your body to secrete endorphins—the feel-good chemicals. That's why a prescription for depression and stress that works as well as pharmaceuticals is to exercise. You make your own "feel-good drugs," and with no nasty side effects.

Do NOT dwell what you were just arguing about! Focus on something else!

A major source of our feelings is what we are mentally focused on at a particular moment. So if you are focusing on something positive like how beautiful the sky and the trees look where you are walking, you're likely to feel better and better. On the other hand, if you focus on whatever unpleasant issues you and your partner were talking about, you are likely to feel worse and worse as your amygdala gets triggered all over again.

Yes, you sincerely want to deal with whatever really needs to be dealt with. But *not now!*

Remember, you don't have much prefrontal cortex intelligence when you're in the middle of an amygdala hijack. Your perception is almost certainly distorted so that you aren't aware of the positives in the situation and the helpful resources you have available. And you have very little creativity to use in generating new approaches to dealing with the situation that are likely to work.

Wait to think further about the situation until later, when you have your full intelligence back. You'll be able to tell when that is because your feeling tone will change: Even though you will still see any problems that really exist, you will have a better feeling. You will begin to see more of the big picture and new possibilities you had not seen previously, so you will feel more confident about your ability to find solutions together that will move your relationship forward.

So do *not* use the break to think about all the things you should have said, what an impossible jerk your partner is, and so on. (At first, those are the thoughts that are most likely to come to mind. So you may need to consciously focus on something else instead.)

"Don't come back until you love him again!"

In his groundbreaking book *Modello: A Story of Hope for the Inner City and Beyond,* Jack Pransky tells the amazing story of a couple of housing units in the Miami area that underwent a remarkable transformation from hotbeds of drugs and drive-by shootings, with children who should have been in school running all over the place, to nurturing communities where murders had ceased and ex-drug dealers were supporting each other in getting a high school education!

A large part of what created the transformation was that the residents gained a new understanding of how their minds work called "Health Realization," now known as "the Three Principles" or "Inside-Out Understanding."

One thing mothers learned to do when they were angry with their children was to take a break. "If you are feeling like hitting your child with a belt and you know you don't really want to do that," they learned, "here's what to do instead. Just put your child in his room and say, 'Don't come out until I come back.' Then go to a neighbor's apartment and talk for a while or watch TV or anything. Just don't think about what you are angry about.

"Don't come back until you feel your love for your child again."

"Don't come back until you feel love for your partner" is good advice for you when you are taking a break, too.

And you can shorten the time you need to be away by consciously thinking about the things that you truly do love about your mate.

While you're taking the break, instead of going over and over what you were just talking about and what your partner said and did, *direct your thoughts to what you like and appreciate about your partner.* (The more you do part "A" of living happily ever the easier you will find this. The ABC's all support each other.)

Ask yourself, "What is one thing I like about (or love about) my partner?" And don't settle for "NOTHING!" If you've been feeling mad at how s/he is treating you, think about what you appreciate about the way s/he is with the kids. Or what s/he did for your birthday. Or how his/her smile warms your heart. Or how s/he makes you laugh even when you're trying to stay mad. The little things, as well as the bigger things.

"What is one small thing you can do?"

Another place to focus your attention (instead of on whatever triggered the Amygdala hijack) is on what you WANT your relationship to be like with this person.

You can ask yourself, "What do I really want in this situation? Not just to get my own way with this current issue, but—what kind of relationship do I want? How do I want us both to treat each other? How do I want us to be feeling about each other?"

Then you can ask yourself a very powerful question:

"What is one small thing I could do to move toward that kind of relationship? What could I do right now to express the kind of relationship I want, to treat this person the way I want us to treat each other?"

When your warm feelings are coming back and you can tell you're on a more even keel, and maybe have in mind "one small thing" you can do to express or move toward the kind of relationship you want, it's time to return.

The spirit with which you do that can make all the difference.

"Hello, Lover!"

The better the feeling with which you begin your next contact, the more likely you are to be able to leave the amygdala hijack behind you.

So the more you can be in touch with being genuinely glad to see your mate again, the better.

If all you can manage is a rueful smile and an "I'm sorry we got into it a bit there," that's fine. If ever there was a moment for a Do-Over, this is it!

Should I apologize?

There's no need to apologize in a way that implies you are to blame for what happened. After all, it took two of you to go off the rails. But your partner will probably appreciate it if you DO express regret that the two of you together got into a hurtful place. "I'm sorry it happened" is different from "I'm sorry I did that to you."

The most important thing is, you don't want to get back into the place you were before the break. The best way to make sure that doesn't happen is to do something else instead.

Don't get back into it. Move on!

Instead of getting right back into the topic you were discussing, you may find it best to bring up another topic—a neutral or positive topic—instead. Ideally, bring up something where you can quickly share some information the other person is likely to be glad to hear ("Annie's grades came in—she got an A in chemistry!") or offer to do something your partner will welcome ("I was thinking—how about if I take the car in to get the oil changed on Saturday?").

You may realize that the amygdala hijack was sparked by something that really doesn't need to be addressed at all. Or you may want to bring up the topic from a different angle, or at a different time, or in a change of setting, like a coffee shop or a park.

Dealing with an Amygdala Hijack

1. Bite your tongue! (Recognize that you're being hijacked—that Mr. Hyde is appearing—and *don't say* what you *know* will make things worse.)

2. Take a break. Instead of escalating, do the amygdala shift. (Disengage, breathe, move, and focus on something else.)

3. Begin again! (Make a graceful, friendly re-entry and move on.)

The break doesn't have to be a long one!

Remember how Ronald Reagan shifted his relationship with Premier Mikhail Gorbachev of the Soviet Union (see Chapter 2)? He actually did all three steps in just a minute or so.

As he and Premier Gorbachev began to raise their voices and get angrier and angrier, at some point President Reagan clearly recognized that the conversation was going off the rails. Whether he knew the term amygdala hijack or not, he saw the signs that things were going downhill. So he did the amygdala shift:

He stopped the action and turned away, as if he was leaving. He didn't suggest taking a break. He just took one!

During the break, he probably took a deep breath and thought about what kind of relationship he DID want with Premier Gorbachev. Then he identified one thing he could do to move toward that kind of relationship.

In this case the break probably took only a few seconds. But it was long enough for President Reagan to be able to turn around with a smile on his face and say, "Let's begin again. My name is Ron. May I call you Mikhail?"

As we've seen, one of the most powerful ways you can use a break to accelerate the move toward getting your intelligence back is by using your breathing. If you'd like to learn a specific breathing technique you can use to relax and de-stress anytime, anywhere, you can download the "Getting My Intelligence Back" technique at www.drkonline.com/dymbonus. It's one of my favorites!

So **A is for** *Appreciation* (look for things to appreciate and tell your partner about them) **and** *Attention* (turn toward your partner, think about your partner, and let your partner know you are thinking about him or her) *and* **Affection** (express some!).

B is for *Break the routine*—whether it's the habitual same old same old or the more dramatic and destructive routine of an amygdala hijack. (In that case you might think of it as *Bite your tongue, take a Break, and Begin again!*)

That brings us to the **C** in the ABC's of living happily ever after. This is the most powerful way to rescue your relationship from The Blahs: *Create a good feeling*.

CHAPTER THIRTEEN

C Is for "Create a Good Feeling"

> *From time to time I ask someone who has had a long and happy marriage, "What is the secret of your success?"*
> *One of the most common answers is some variation of "We just have fun together!"*

Perhaps the biggest difference between dating and a relationship suffering from The Blahs is that dating is *all about* having a good time together. When you're dating, you are constantly thinking about what would be fun to do with each other, what your partner would probably enjoy, what *you* would probably enjoy doing together—and going and *doing* it.

After they're "together" and no longer dating, many couples completely stop thinking about how to have fun together. Their focus is no longer on having fun, but on just getting through the day—doing all the things that need to be done to keep a household running. Maybe they sit down next to each other and watch some TV, or maybe they even go out to a movie, but that is more about recovering from the stress of the day than about having fun together.

This is a big mistake, and it's a big source of The Blahs.

The couples who live happily ever after make it a priority to keep on having a good time together.

Remember "positive sentiment override?"

Consistently creating a good feeling is about more than just having fun once in awhile. It can set the tone for the whole relationship.

Remember the researchers we learned about in Chapter Four who discovered negative and positive sentiment override—that some couples miss most of the positive things that their partners do and concentrate on the negative, while other couples do the reverse?

Happy couples *live* in positive sentiment override. That's a big part of why they stay together, and it's a big part of what makes them happy.

How does positive sentiment override come about?

We learned that part of the answer is that happy couples make a point of noticing things to appreciate about their partner and their relationship—and then telling their partners what they have noticed and how much they do appreciate it.

But that's not all.

Velcro or Teflon?

The happy couples actually decide to reverse our brain's wired-in tendency to pay more attention to the negative. They intentionally pay more attention to whatever is positive in their relationship and let the rest go.

They're not in denial. It's not that the happy couples pretend nothing negative ever happens, but they *decide* to become Teflon to that and Velcro to the positive. They simply don't dwell on the negative. When they think of something negative about the relationship or their partner, they dismiss the thought and focus on something else. They don't treat it as something important. If the negative thought keeps coming back, *they deal with anything that can be dealt with and then forget about it.* They just move on to something else.

Yes, deal with the things that really need to be addressed. But then put them behind you.

At the same time, *they are actively looking for the positive. When they notice something, they take a moment to enjoy it.* These thoughts they do dwell on. And because of the way our brains work, the more the happy couples look for and pay attention to the positive, the more positive they see. And each time they see something positive, they feel good about it. This is one of the subtle ways happy couples create a good feeling. You can do this too.

Taking a break from the negative

This is also part of why "taking a break" can help your relationship thrive.

Doing the same old thing over and over can get really boring. Whatever you do to break the routine feels better. Bingo! Another contribution to positive sentiment override.

Even more powerful, when you take a break as soon as an amygdala hijack starts you are making sure you and your partner spend less time in and less focus on negative states of mind. Less time in the negative—more time feeling good. It all adds up.

What would we both enjoy?

The biggest contribution you can make to living in positive sentiment override is also the most fun.

Take a tip from the happy couples: Make it a priority to think regularly about what you would both enjoy doing. Then carve out time in your busy schedules to go and *do* it!

The ways you can do things you enjoy together are limited only by your imagination and your creativity—and you can develop both by using them. Let's explore a few ways other couples have created a good feeling.

CHAPTER FOURTEEN

A Carillon Playing Chopin?!

The basic idea is very simple and can be a lot of fun: Make time to do things you enjoy—*together!*

It may be simple, but it's not easy!

You'd think it would come naturally to make sure we have a good time together, and in a way it does.

Nobody has to teach us how to do that when we're dating. Why are things so different after the honeymoon?

We get busy.

While we're dating, we're on one of the most important quests human beings ever embark on, driven by an urge wired into our DNA: Find a mate.

"Making time" to do that is simply not an issue.

And the activities that are part of that quest are exactly the things that feel so good about dating: seeking out and spending time with an attractive member of the opposite sex. Thinking of and doing things we hope our partner will enjoy. Talking about the things that are really important to us, with someone who is an eager audience and shares deeply with us in return. Being with someone who is interested in getting to know us, discovering our likes and dislikes, our opinions on things, what makes us tick. Someone who enjoys our sense of humor. And, crucially, while we're together, we are focused not on other concerns in our lives, but on each other. "I only have eyes for you."

After the honeymoon those other concerns take center stage.

"Time to go to work." "Could you take the baby? I've got to make dinner." "In the high wind some shingles blew off the roof. You'd better do something about it."

There's too much to do, and too little time to do it all. It's not easy finding time to simply be together, never mind doing things "just for fun."

But *finding that time is not just a "nice to do." It's a "must do" if you want your marriage to survive and thrive.*

Because having a good time together is the best prevention and the best cure for The Blahs.

The Blahs are no fun

More than anything else, that's what The Blahs ARE: a relationship that isn't fun any more—that feels like an endless treadmill you're stuck on instead of a joyous ride or adventurous journey you're taking together. So the best way to get off the treadmill and defeat The Blahs is to get back to doing things you enjoy together *even though it's hard to find the time.* That's what the couples who live happily ever after do. Even when they're crazy busy, they make sure they take time to do things together that they enjoy. They make it a top priority, not something to do "if they get around to it."

You can do that too.

"But what do we DO?"

When I tell couples who come to see me or work with me via Skype that the best way out of The Blahs is to start having more fun together, they sometimes give me a blank look. More often than you might expect, one of them will say something like, "But what do we DO?"

If you're out of the habit of making time just for doing things you enjoy together, you may wonder the same thing.

Well, what did you do when you were dating?

Did you go out dancing? Go to an amusement park? Take long walks together?

Start there.

What *have* you done that you've enjoyed since you got married? Do that!

Then branch out.

What have you wanted to try?

What are some things you don't *know* you'll enjoy but expect you might? A great way to Break the routine is to surprise your mate with an activity neither one of you has ever tried.

> *For years I've loved to play ultimate frisbee (a game kind of like soccer but played with a flying disc), but I had never played disc golf (which is, as you might expect, a game like GOLF but played with a flying disc!). I thought it would be fun to see what it's like.*
>
> *So one Wednesday or Thursday recently I said, "I've got something in mind for Sunday afternoon. Could we leave about 3 and be back a little after sunset?"*
>
> *Kari very reasonably asked, "What is it?" I answered, "It's a surprise." (I know she likes surprises.) "She grinned. "OK, what shall I wear?" "Just be dressed for being outside. Not fancy, roughing it."*
>
> *When we got in the car on Sunday afternoon, Kari asked, "Where are we going?" I've learned that even though she asks, she really likes to not know. It makes it more of an adventure. So I just said, "You'll see."*
>
> *I took her to a park at the very bottom of the peninsula we live on, in St. Petersburg, Florida. The area is beautiful, with a small beach and a couple of boat launching ramps on a pretty waterway. But we weren't going to the beach. I had sought out the park on Google because it has a disc golf course.*

> We parked and I got a couple of frisbees out of the trunk. "Are we going to toss?" Kari asked. "Wait a minute—why do you have TWO frisbees?" "You'll see," I said, and we walked to the first tee. I explained what we were about to do. (A disc golf course is a lot like a regular golf course: you start from a designated tee, throw your frisbee down a long fairway, sometimes with obstacles like water hazards, and end by throwing it into a special basket - the "hole.") We started off taking turns throwing our frisbees.
>
> After several throws, we both managed to get our frisbees into the first hole.
>
> Neither of us was much good at it. But that wasn't the point. We had a great time! Every couple of holes Kari said, "This is FUN! I'm so glad you did this!"
>
> We ended the day with a picnic I had prepared, sitting in a shelter at the edge of the beach, watching the sun go down.
>
> Feeling a good feeling, together.

Go on an "Expotition!"

That wasn't the first time I had suggested we do something without saying what we were going to do.

My freshman year at Oberlin College, a group of friends met every morning in the cafeteria to read from the books by A. A. Milne about Winnie the Pooh. One of my favorite ideas came from learning that Pooh and his friends sometimes went on "Expotitions" to explore the world. I began doing that with my friends.

> When Kari and I moved to Colorado, I suggested we start going on Sunday afternoon Expotitions to get to know our new surroundings. We had fun doing it, so we started going on Expotitions again when we moved to Florida.
>
> At first we didn't know where to go, besides the theme parks. So I asked my friend Rich, who had lived in Florida for years, what he would suggest. "Do you know about One Tank

Trips?" he asked? I didn't. Rich explained that there had been a TV show for years about interesting places to go in Florida that would take a tank of gas or less from the Tampa area where we live. He thought there was a book based on the TV series.

It turns out there is actually a whole series of books, each with brief descriptions of 52 One Tank Trips. Everything from museums to art festivals to mini-golf with live alligators (in ponds, not playing mini-golf). Enough ideas for years of Expotitions.

Our favorite one tank trip so far was to Bok Tower.

The tower was built on one of the highest points in Florida (a majestic 298 feet!) and is beautifully landscaped, surrounded by amazing flower gardens. But for us the best part is that the tower contains a carillon. Intrigued, I Googled Bok Tower and found out that they have evening carillon concerts every month at the full moon. Perfect for an Expotition!

As I expected, Kari was delighted when she found out where we had been heading. But both of us were blown away by the concert. The man playing the carillon, Geert D'hollander, is one of the best in the world. We were astonished to hear him playing Chopin's E-Flat Nocturne and Military Polonaise, Solveg's Song, and many other classical pieces, with full expression—on the carillon bells!

Whether classical music played on carillon bells or mini-golf with alligators is more your style, you too can find ways to Break your routine and Create a good feeling that will strengthen your relationship and enrich your lives. Just ask around!

It doesn't HAVE to take a lot of time!

By the way, what contributes the most to your relationship is not how much time you spend but the fact that you are making it a priority to create a good feeling together. A warm smile as you look into each other's eyes when you pass on the way to the bathroom or texting a photo you snapped with your iPhone camera when you saw something beautiful or just calling "to say I love you" only takes a few seconds.

But the good feeling you create for yourself and your mate can make all the difference.

For a quick way to generate a good feeling, think together about some things you would both like to do—and then plan to do them.

If you'd like a worksheet with some questions and ideas to get you started, go and check out "What Can We Do For Fun?" at www.drkonline.com/dymbonus.

CHAPTER FIFTEEN

"You're special!"

> *Sometimes I ask people what they enjoyed most about dating. One person said, "Getting dressed up! When I'd go out on a date, I always went out of my way to look my best—and so did my date. It made the whole evening magical. Especially the first moment we saw each other when he picked me up!"*

A subtle contributor to The Blahs is that after the honeymoon we too often stop making our time together special.

Even if we do religiously observe "date night," we just get to the end of whatever we're doing, say, "Are you ready to go?" and head out, still wearing whatever we were already wearing and probably still thinking about whatever we were already thinking about.

Think how this contributes to the feeling of "same old routine!"

You're worth getting dressed up for!

What is the message when we DO we make a special effort to get dressed up? We're telling the people we are going to meet, "You are special. This event is special." Not surprisingly, we feel a bit special ourselves.

It's a powerful message to your mate when you take the trouble to look especially nice before going out together.

You're saying, "You're special. You're worth getting dressed up for!"

A hassle—or a gift?

When I talk about this idea, some people say, "That sounds like such a hassle! When I'm going out to have fun with my partner, I don't want to have to go to all that trouble. I just want to relax!"

"Fair enough," I answer. But what if at least once in a while, instead of seeing it as something you *"have to"* do, you think of it as a gift you're giving your partner? Or maybe you plan an "Expotition" to a place where dressing up will add to the fun? (Warn your partner about it in advance so s/he's not caught by surprise.)

An added advantage of planning it in advance is that your mate is less likely to be too distracted even to notice if *you* get dressed up!

Use "pet names"

A lot of people spontaneously start calling each other by special pet names when they're dating. "Honey," Sweetheart," and so on or something more personal.

The more personal it is, the more fun it can be.

> *One day I asked Kari what she'd like to be called that would make her feel special. She said, "try a few on me." So I made a list.*
>
> *The ones she decided she liked best were "Honeysuckle" and "Morning Glory."*
>
> *I still mostly call her "Honey" (she said she likes that too), but every so often I call her Morning Glory or Honeysuckle.*
>
> *When I do, she always gives a contented little sigh that makes my heart flutter.*

How else can you say, "You're special?"

Remember what you did when you were dating? That kind of thing.

Bring home a bunch of flowers from a florist's or the supermarket—or wildflowers you picked on the way home. Or take it up a level. Have flowers delivered.

Bring a small gift that shows you were thinking of your mate. A special treat to eat. A candle to burn at bedtime or as you take a bath together. (Haven't done that in a while? Ever? Try it! Bubble bath is even more fun!)

Mail your mate an invitation to your next "Expotition" Hand-drawn is fine, or it's easy to print one from your computer: Google "free invitation template." For a really special anniversary, send your mate an ENGRAVED invitation from a print shop!

As I suggested before, make a hand-done "World's Best Spouse" certificate. Just like a little kid would draw! (Hint: The clunkier it looks, the more it will touch your mate's heart!)

Remember the "A" of living happily after? The main thing here is that you're expressing your Affection and Appreciation for your mate by paying Attention to that wonderful person. Taking time from your busy schedule to do something special *with* your mate or *for* your mate is how you *tell* your mate s/he's special. And there are few better ways to "Create a good feeling."

For a worksheet to help you generate ideas you can use to make your mate feel special, go and download "You're Special!" at www.drkonline.com/dymbonus.

There's something else you can do that will not only make your partner feel special, it will help you stay in touch with and even deepen what *is* special about your partner.

CHAPTER SIXTEEN

"Talk to me!"

"I've been happily married for 29 years."
"That's great. What's the secret of your success?"
"Well, in my previous marriage..."
Oh, you were married before?"
"Oh yes. In my previous marriage, when my wife would say 'Let's talk,' I was like, 'NOW? Fifteen minutes before the end of Columbo?!'

"Now I turn off the television."

The number one complaint of many couples who come to see me is "communication problems." When I ask what they mean by communication problems, a surprising number of people say, "We have NO communication. We never talk."

Of course, that's usually not literally true.

Most couples do talk from time to time. Sometimes they talk many times a day.

But what they talk about is mainly practical matters—the logistics and arrangements of living.

"We're out of eggs." "What else do I need to get at the store?"

"Jimmy has basketball practice after school. Can you pick him up?"

"The front door is sticking. I think it's the change in humidity. Could you do something about it?"

As we explore further, it usually becomes clear that when people say, "We never talk," they mean, "We aren't talking about the important things. We aren't doing the kind of communicating that makes us feel close."

How different things are when most couples are dating!

"FINALLY! Someone who UNDERSTANDS me!"

Do you remember what it was like when you first met your mate? If you're like many couples, you talked for hours. In fact, that may have been what first signaled that this was someone special. The first or second time you spent time with each other, you may have begun by meeting casually at a party or having a meal together and realized suddenly that hours had gone by and you were still talking animatedly and no one else was around!

At last—maybe for the first time!—you felt you had met someone who really understood you, who shared your interest in and enthusiasm for things that other people didn't seem to "get."

You were fascinated to learn the littlest things about your partner's background and life experiences. And your partner was just as interested in learning those things about you.

Many couples find that this mutual sharing is one of the most powerful factors that quickly build intimacy when they first meet.

And it's one of the things they miss most when they become distracted by other concerns and "too busy to talk" as The Blahs settle in.

Give each other the time of day

It doesn't have to be that way. Dr. Gottman and other researchers have found that the happy couples—the ones whose marriages continue to flourish and grow—keep talking together. And not just about who will pick up Janie after her music lessons.

They continue to ask each other about their day and how things are going. And they don't expect or settle for "Oh, you know, same old same-old" as an answer. They tell each other the little things that happened. The minor frustrations or amusing surprises or small triumphs.

And they talk about the bigger things too, updating their maps of their partner's inner world.

"How is it different for you now that you got that promotion at work? Are people treating you differently? Are you feeling differently about yourself?"

"You know, realizing that my 40th birthday is coming up feels kind of weird. I remember when I was a kid, 40 seemed so OLD..."

"Been there? Done that?"

When I first talk about this kind of communication with the couples who come to see me, many say something like, "I don't know what to talk about! I mean, it was easy when we were dating, because we didn't know each other then. Everything we learned was new. Now we know each other so well, I can usually predict what he's going to say before he says it! There's nothing new to say or hear!"

I tell them what Judy, a participant in one of my workshops, said about that:

> "We live right near the beach," she said. "Many days we go to watch the sun go down. So do a lot of our neighbors.
>
> "It seems to me that saying there's nothing new to learn about my spouse would be like someone saying, 'Why would

you bother to watch the sunset after you've done it once? You KNOW what's going to happen. It's going to go down! Been there, done that. BOORRRING!'

"But of course it's NOT boring. The sunset is different every day. You just need to notice the differences.

"I think your spouse is the same way: different every day. You just need to be interested enough to notice the differences!"

Beyond "women's liberation"

One of the biggest sources of divorce is that one partner—often the woman—has changed. The partner hasn't kept up. Sometimes the partner hasn't even noticed! (Or has noticed and is threatened by the change so he tries to squash it.) During the decades when "women's liberation" was a big news item, many women woke up to the life-deadening effects of the cultural straitjackets both men and women were raised to put on. Many of their partners haven't really waked up to that yet.

In other cases, perhaps through travel associated with his job, a man has found that his horizons have broadened and his wife is being left behind. They don't seem to have as much in common as they once did.

Talking about the things that matter instead of just day-to-day logistics can help to bridge the gap. It can also provide real depth and a whole new kind of joy, satisfaction, and connection—a new kind of relationship.

Interestingly When John Gottman first taught couples about what his research showed about activities that could strengthen their marriages, he didn't include talking together. But he discovered when he followed up with the couples he had taught that the ones who had benefited most from what they learned had nearly all invented for themselves what he came to call a "stress-reducing conversation." Just about every day, they would sit down together for 20 minutes or so and "just talk," catching each other up on their day and what they were thinking about. And as the name suggests, many of the couples reported that a nice side benefit of these conversations was a reduction of the stress they were feeling in their lives.

Go easy on the advice!

There's one thing to watch out for: instead of reducing stress, talking can actually *add* stress if one person (usually a man) responds to his mate's expression of frustration or concern about something by telling her what she should have done or what she should do about it. Mainly, what reduces stress for most women is simply being heard and understood and empathized with—unless or until she ASKS for advice.

Your own "stress-reducing conversations"

One of the best ways to "date your mate" is to spend time often—maybe every day—"just talking." The only rule is, no "business" talk. You can talk about anything else, but this time is NOT for making arrangements about practical matters needed to keep the ship afloat. And it's not a time for trying to solve "problems" in your relationship, either.

This time is for dreaming, for catching each other up on what you have been thinking or feeling, for sharing experiences from your past that (even after all your time together!) the other has never heard about. For sharing your ideas about what you would like to add to your life together, or what you want your future to hold.

As you talk, you will continue to see sides of the other person you've never seen before. Your understanding of each other and your connection will become richer and richer.

What is going on in your life, or your spouse's life, that could give one of you a fresh insight into the other? "Getting to know" a person is a never-ending quest, and can be a lifelong delight. Keep looking—and keep talking!

For more ideas of how to save your relationship from The Blahs by talking together, download the "Happy Talk" technique at *www.drkonline.com/dymbonus*.

All this may sound great, but you may be wondering, "How will I ever remember to *do* all these things to Create a good feeling—and for that matter, how will I remember to do all the other things happy couples do—to Break the routine and to give my relationship and my mate the Attention and Appreciation and Affection that I know will make a big difference?"

Fortunately, help is close at hand: Your reptilian brain is available to help you to tap in to the power of *ritual*.

CHAPTER SEVENTEEN

Bang Bang Shrimp: the Power of Rituals

Some of the things you do to express appreciation and give attention to your partner just happen once, and breaking out of routines that have become boring is part of how dating your mate can save your relationship from The Blahs.

Paradoxically, however, another wonderful part of dating is CREATING routines—rituals that have special meaning to the two of you.

What do you mean, "creating" rituals?

There is a part of us—our "reptilian brain"—that LIKES routine as long as it feels good. (Think of a lizard on a rock basking in the sun, or how good it can feel to soak in a luxurious hot bath. Think how mesmerizing it can be to tap your foot to a regular drumbeat.)

Rituals add depth and meaning to our lives. Whether the ritual of getting together for religious services or holidays or special ways of celebrating birthdays and wedding and other life passages, the rituals we participate in are a major source of richness for all of us.

But the idea of creating rituals on purpose is a new one for many people. We just accept the rituals our culture offers us—the ones we grew up with—and that is that.

Sometimes we enjoy them and find meaning in them, other times we feel we are just going through meaningless motions or even feel stuck spending time doing things we don't see the point of doing with people we don't enjoy.

When two people form a relationship, they inherit two sets of rituals: the ones each person experienced in their life before they met each other.

A wonderful way to add depth and good feeling to your relationship is to spend some time thinking about which rituals feel like excess baggage, which you love, and which areas of your life are "ritual-poor," where you want to invent rituals that will be meaningful for you.

Some rituals take almost no time but bring immediate pleasure—like using pet names for each other or greeting each other in a special way.

Other rituals involve pleasurable activities that take more time—like talking together about topics that deepen your emotional connection.

A bedtime ritual isn't just for children!

> When our daughter Lyrica was young, we heard many parents complaining about how hard it was to get their children to go to bed when it was "bedtime." We never experienced that with Lyrica, and I believe it was because she always looked forward to our bedtime ritual.
>
> From the time Lyrica was tiny, when evening came we would start a candle burning in her room and turn off the lights. That was the signal that it was bedtime. Next would come a bath, which she always enjoyed. Then when she was all dried off and in her nightgown, we'd put her in her bed. As she snuggled in to the soft covers, we would rub her back, and then read to her for a few minutes as she drifted off to sleep.

Lyrica has now moved away and become a parent herself. But one of my favorite rituals with my wife Kari is still reading to each other. When we are on a car trip, whichever one of us isn't driving often reads aloud to the one who is driving.

On the other hand, we've evolved a bedtime ritual that just goes one way. I read Kari to sleep.

> *It began when I became aware of the Harry Potter books. I started to read the first one to see what all the fuss was about and quickly got hooked. I thought it would be fun to share with Kari, so I started at the beginning, reading it to her after she was in bed. She liked it, so I read some more the next night.*
>
> *By then she was hooked too, and we kept on going until we finished the book. Then she suggested we read the next one, and I thought that was a great idea. So we did.*
>
> *I was doing a lot of business traveling at the time, but we continued the ritual. I would call her from a hotel to give her the hotel phone number, then she would call me back and I would read her to sleep. It felt especially good to be connected that way when I was at a distance.*
>
> *At some point we caught up with Rowling and had to wait for the next book in the series to come out. We started reading another series until the next Harry Potter book was available.*
>
> *I've been reading to Kari just about every night ever since.*
>
> *Mostly we've read young adult fantasy series like the Eregon series and Rick* Riordan's *Percy Jackson and the Olympians series. But right now we're also reading a wonderful book Kari's sister Judy recommended,* The 100 Year Old Man Who Climbed Out A Window And Disappeared.
>
> *Along the way I discovered that Kari often fell asleep and missed several pages, so I would have to go back and read them again. So I started asking "Are you still awake?" Then she got to where she could wake up enough to answer "yes" and go right back to sleep.*

So then I began asking her questions about what I have just read. When she can't answer them, I know it's time to stop!

Holiday Rituals

A favorite for many couples are special holiday rituals. These are frequently times that the extended family gathers to create good feeling together.

The thing is, we often just fall into doing things a certain way around the holidays because our parents did—whether we really enjoy them or not.

A good thing to talk about together is what holidays were special for you when you were growing up, and how each of your families celebrated them.

Then talk about which elements of those celebrations you'd like to try out, to see if they or some version of them will add enjoyment to your life together now.

If neither of your families had a ritual you enjoyed connected with a holiday that you would like to celebrate, you can *make up* a ritual—a way of celebrating that would be fun for you.

Spiritual Rituals

Many holidays have religious overtones or celebrate religious events. (After all, the word "holiday" comes from "holy day!") And most religions are loaded with rituals that help make believers' lives more meaningful.

What are some of your favorite spiritual rituals? A weekly religious service? Saying grace when you begin a meal? Praying together at certain times every day? Marking your children's passage from childhood to adulthood or other of life passages in a special way with other members of your faith?

All these and more can add depth and meaning to the good feeling you are creating together.

Why is that particular road paved with "good intentions?"

We're creatures of habit much more than we might like to believe. So when we learn something new, even if it seems like something we'd like to continue, we often don't. Instead, we just do it for a little while and then it drops away. Our old habits take over, and soon we're living just as we were before we learned it.

WATCH OUT! This is very likely to happen with all the great ideas you've gotten while you've been reading this book about what you could do to make your relationship better.

You'll do something once, maybe twice. Both of you will enjoy it and one of you will say, "We've got to do this again."

But you won't. Or maybe you'll do it once more. Then in a year or so one of you will say, "Things were really nice while we were reading that *Date Your Mate* book. I wonder what happened. . . "

But habits can cut both ways. Once you've made something you want to add to your life into a habit, it has a momentum of its own. As we saw in Chapter 5, once you've made it through "habit gravity" and reached liftoff, a habit can actually help you do the things you otherwise wouldn't get around to.

Rituals can be a powerful tool for bridging the gap between "my habit is NOT to do it" and "now my habit is TO do it."

Invent new rituals to create new habits!

Say you've decided you like the idea of breaking the routine by calling or texting your spouse to suggest an unplanned lunch together or a walk in the park after work. Here's a ritual you can establish to make sure you get around to being "spontaneous":

> *Set a weekly alarm on your smart phone or desk clock to remind you at the same time every week to take a moment, look ahead, and plan a couple of times over the next few days to call or text your spouse with a "Break the Routine" suggestion. Then set alarms to go off at those times.*
>
> *When one of the alarms you've set for "breaking the routine" goes off, make up something to do and then contact your spouse and suggest it.*
>
> *So the **ritual** is weekly planning time—to plan for spontaneity!*

Or say you like the idea of going on special "Expotitions" together.

> *You can establish a ritual that these happen every two weeks or once a month on, say, Sunday afternoon and that you'll take turns initiating them, so if your spouse chose the one you're currently doing, as soon as it's over it's your turn to come up with the next one.*
>
> *If you like, once again, you can create an alarm-driven "planning ritual" to make sure it happens.*

Almost anything the two of you enjoy can become a ritual. That's where the title of this chapter came from.

Bang Bang shrimp

There's a restaurant chain called Bonefish Grill. A favorite dish of mine at Bonefish Grill is a delicacy they call Bang Bang shrimp.

When I was building my relationship coaching practice, every time I got a new client Kari and I would go out for Bang Bang shrimp. Whenever something really special happens, we still do.

For some more ideas about how you can create a good feeling by adding rituals to your life together, download "Creating Rituals" at www.drkonline.com/dymbonus.

There's a secret built in to rituals like these that you can use to create more joy and satisfaction everywhere in your life. It has to do with a brain chemical called dopamine.

CHAPTER EIGHTEEN

Something to Look Forward to

One of the reasons that enjoyable rituals can have such a powerful impact on your relationship is because of a special way that our brains create pleasure.

> *If you grew up in a home where Christmas was celebrated (or another holiday that involved giving and receiving presents), remember what it was like on Christmas Eve (or before the presents were opened)? Remember how excited you felt?*
> *Now think about what it was like Christmas DAY—after all the presents had been opened. It was nice having what you had been given, of course. But can you remember that there was a little bit of a letdown?*

That shift in how you felt came about because the pleasure that you feel when you get something you wanted comes from a neurotransmitter called serotonin. And serotonin does feel good.

But the pleasure you get from anticipation is from dopamine—a different neurotransmitter that powers an entirely different pleasure system. And the pleasure from anticipation is much more exciting.

This is why people who have worked hard for a long time to achieve something may find themselves feeling a little let down after they get it. This is the "Is this all there is?" feeling.

It's because, nice as the serotonin is, it's not dopamine.

What they MISS is the dopamine.

When the Dopamine is Gone . . .

Some people say that men get less interested in their wives after they get married because the conquest is gone. "I got you." While this may sometimes be true, I believe that a bigger factor is this: while they're dating, men are feeling dopamine—the anticipation of being together. Once they *are* together, the dopamine is gone!

But you can put dopamine back into your relationship.

The way you do it is, *make sure that you and your mate always have something to look forward to.*

And building enjoyable rituals into your life is one way to have something to look forward to.

I'll tell you WHEN we're going, but I won't tell you WHERE!

You can add this quality of having something to look forward to even to a predictable routine.

This is what I do when I tell Kari when we will go on an "Expotition" but don't tell her where we're going until we get there. She enjoys it twice as much because of the building anticipation.

This is also part of why a ritual of giving presents on certain occasions works so well: You know there's going to be *something* but you don't know *what*—so even though you know when the presents will be given, there's still a lot of anticipation.

(This is also why it works so well to *wrap* presents: Seeing a present right in front of you but still not knowing what it is adds to the anticipation—and the dopamine continues to build as you take the time to unwrap the present.)

One of the most powerful secrets to Creating a good feeling in your relationship, as to having an enjoyable and fulfilling life, is this:

Always have something to look forward to
My friend Robert Fritz, an expert in the creative process, once revealed a secret that helps explain why many prolific artists are able to stay so productive year after year. "The most successful artists," he said, "nearly always start one or two new art works *before* they complete the one they're working on. That way as soon as one work is done, their creativity has somewhere else to flow—and they already are beginning to build excitement about the new work."

So make sure you and your mate always have something to look forward to—and keep the dopamine flowing!

CHAPTER NINETEEN

"One More Thing. . ."

A smiling, vibrant woman who came to one of my talks said,
"I'm about to celebrate my 52nd anniversary. And I'd have to say we are one of your "happy couples." I asked her what she considered her secret of success.
"A lot of the things you've been talking about," she answered. "But especially date night. We've hardly missed a week since we got married."
"And," she added. "Keeping God at the center of our marriage."

That's worth mentioning. It's not something John Gottman picked up on, because the couples in his research were from all faiths and no faith. But many of the happiest couples I've asked about what contributed to their long-lasting, satisfying relationships have mentioned that a spiritual connection of one kind or another was an important element in their marriage.

So when I speak of Creating a good feeling, I'm talking about more than superficial pleasure, although that is certainly helpful in keeping a relationship alive.

I'm also talking about a deeper "good feeling" that nourishes body, heart, mind—and soul.

Opening to Love

Whether you talk about God or use some other language, most people would agree that we're not running the show. We don't make the seasons change or the sun come up or create the natural beauty and the love that tugs at our hearts.

Most people would agree that love is one of the most powerful forces in the universe. Maybe the most powerful. Some say it is even the same attractive force that keeps atoms together and planets circling the stars.

One of the greatest opportunities we have to tap into something deeper—to align with whatever it is that makes the stars shine and gives us life—is experiencing the love that flows when we open fully to each other.

And one of the ways we can most deeply find and connect with each other is to open to God, to the Life Force—to open to Love.

CHAPTER TWENTY

"Surprise!"

So: we've talked about three powerful ways you can save your relationship from The Blahs and greatly increase your chances of having a satisfying relationship that lasts and gets better with every passing year: *The ABC's of living happily ever after.*

A is for Appreciation and Attention—and Affection.

We've talked about how Attention is the fuel relationships run on.

We've learned how it's natural to notice what's negative and miss what is positive about our mate and our relationship, and how we can make a point of appreciating and telling our mate what we appreciate instead.

We've noted how appreciating our mates and what they do and paying attention to our mates both express and strengthen our affection for each other.

B is for Break the routine, and also for Bite your tongue, take a Break, and Begin again.

We have explored how deadening it is to settle into too much of a routine, and how we can enliven our relationship by breaking out of that routine.

We have learned how our brains can fool us into thinking things are worse than they are and make us feel that it's urgent to do things we'll later regret during an amygdala hijack—and we know what we can do to recognize that we are being hijacked, make an amygdala shift, and get our intelligence back.

C is for Create a good feeling.

We have learned how essential it is to create a good feeling as the foundation of our relationship that makes everything else work better (and we've noticed how challenging it can be to take the time needed to create that good feeling when our lives become busy!).

We have explored how to make time for what we enjoy doing together, and how to make our activities and our partners feel special.

We have recognized the importance of "just talking" together, and the value of creating rituals to add depth and meaning and "something to look forward to" to our lives.

Putting it all together!

In closing, I'd like to share with you one of my favorite examples of how someone simultaneously did A and B and C and thereby both banished The Blahs and added a special boost to how he ands wife are living happily ever after.

My friend Bob changed my marriage and my life when he told me about something he did one evening—and his wife's reaction.

> Bob noticed that the kitchen was a mess. His wife was working in her office, and he decided to surprise her by giving the kitchen a special cleaning.
>
> He did the dishes and put them away. He washed all the pots and pans that had accumulated, dried them, and put them away. He washed out the kitchen sink with scouring powder and made it gleam—even the strainer basket in the drain. He took everything off the counters, did a thorough cleaning, then put things back neatly, washing off smudges on the canisters so they sparkled too.
>
> Then he swept and mopped the floor.
>
> He took out the trash.
>
> He wiped the fronts of all the cabinets, the dishwasher, the stove, and the refrigerator.
>
> When Bob was done, the kitchen looked like a photo in an architectural magazine. Then he went to his wife's office and said he had a surprise for her.
>
> She grinned and said, "What is it?"
>
> Bob just said, "Come and see!" and led her to the kitchen.

Her response was what changed my marriage:

> As soon as she walked into the kitchen, Bob's wife stopped, with her mouth open. Then she said, "That is the sexiest thing I've ever seen!"

Not "nicest." SEXIEST!

When I told my wife Kari the story, she said, "Well, of course! When you know your husband is noticing what it takes to keep a home running, and he pitches in and does some of the work without being asked, that is VERY sexy! It opens up your heart!"

I never would have guessed.

Then I heard John Gottman speak once, and he referred to the same principle and expanded on it. He said, *"Every positive thing you do in your relationship is foreplay!"*

Learning this—learning ALL of what I've shared with you—has changed my marriage.

I hope you'll use it to change your relationship as well!

For one last bonus building on this idea of how sexy Bob's wife found his surprise kitchen cleanup, download "Unusual Foreplay" at www.drkonline.com/dymbonus.

CHAPTER TWENTY-ONE

I Hope This Isn't the End!

As Humphrey Bogart says at the end of the movie Casablanca,
"This could be the beginning of a beautiful relationship!"

Please help me spread the word!

I'm on a quest to let as many people as possible know the good news—that "Happily Ever After" is not just a fairy tale, but a real possibility for people in the real world. And it isn't that hard!

I aim to do all I can to make sure that the next generation of children grow up knowing the real potential of love and satisfaction and happiness that is available to them when they find a mate, because they've grown up in a family with parents who are showing them the way, experiencing that love and joy and satisfaction every day.

I need and would deeply appreciate your helping me make that happen. If you'd like to help spread the word, here are a few ways you can do it:

1) **Go to Amazon.com and leave a review for** *Date Your Mate*, telling people about your experience with the book and how they might find it helpful. *(Reading reviews is one of the main ways people decide which books to buy! If you do nothing else, please do this.*

It will take you five minutes or so and can make a huge difference. You can even do it right now! Thanks!)

2) **Give copies of the book to friends and relatives** you think would enjoy reading the book and find it useful. (If you just tell them about the book, they may or may not get around to getting it. If you give it to them, there's a good chance they will read it!)

3) **Form a book club or study circle.** Get together with a bunch of friends or start a Meetup to read the book (perhaps read it aloud!) and **then share experiences and ideas for how you can apply it** to your own relationships.

If something comes up. . .

You now know how to build a solid foundation for a great relationship. Still, you're just beginning to put your new insights into practice. You may not have developed the ability yet to keep from getting derailed when emotional obstacles arise. If you want help developing that ability, I'm here. I'd love to give you a hand.

Please contact me and let me know how you use what you learn here—or with any questions you have about how to make it work for you. You can reach me at DrK@DrKOnline.com

---

I look forward to hearing from you, and—if we haven't already—to one day meeting in person.

Warm regards,
Kalen Hammann/Dr. K

Actually, there's one more thing I want to share with you now . . .

CHAPTER TWENTY-TWO

Afterword: "But what about. . ."

As you've been reading this book, you've probably noticed a glaring omission:

I haven't said a word about how to deal with the often frustrating and bewildering *differences* that frequently get in the way of all the good feeling I've been talking about. I haven't said a word about CONFLICT—about what to do when one of you wants one thing and the other wants something different *and you can't do both!*

In many cases, these differences are what give rise to the feelings of being threatened and powerless that trigger an amygdala hijack.

In other cases, these differences can sometimes make you wonder whether no matter how much you often enjoy being together, you really belong with this person at all.

I haven't talked about any of that because I've learned that it probably wouldn't have helped. There were some other things you needed to learn first.

Here's why.

Knowing how to handle "the bad stuff" is not enough!

When I was first working with couples as a psychologist in Massachusetts I assumed that the most important way I could help would be to address the pain the people were feeling and the problems they were experiencing due to all the challenging differences between them. So I got pretty good at helping people learn how to deal productively with those differences.

And sometimes it helped a lot.

But more often it didn't.

I was bewildered and confused. I had assumed that if we could get the dysfunctional conflict out of a relationship, then people's innate health would simply surface and the rest would be clear sailing for them.

It turned out not to be true.

When I read about John Gottman's research, I finally understood why: Most couples who are miserable in their relationships don't just need to know how to deal with their differences.

They also need to develop new habits that will build a solid foundation for their relationship—a foundation they never built because they didn't do spontaneously what the happy couples do without thinking about it.

You can't build a house beginning with the second floor.

I came to understand that without that foundation in place, even the helpful techniques and communication skills I taught them for dealing with their differences weren't so helpful. *They often didn't trust each other enough and feel good enough about each other to use them!*

It was as if I had been trying to help them build a house beginning with the second floor.

I came to realize that *before* people can deal well with their differences, they need to have a solid foundation of good feeling in place—good feeling about each other and good feeling about the relationship. They need to be living in positive sentiment override.

So I decided to write this book to help you and others like you build that foundation.

But *this isn't the end of learning to live happily ever after. It's really the beginning.*

Now you're ready . . .

Now that you know how to build a foundation of good feeling (and have at least made a beginning at applying and practicing what you've been learning), you are in a position to learn how to deal with your differences in ways that build closeness instead of tearing you apart.

As you do, you'll find that you are at last building together a relationship you truly love. A relationship that is deeply satisfying and fulfilling now and grows to be more and more wonderful with the passage of time—in ways you can only begin to imagine!

How to do that is the topic of my next book, *Don't Get Mad, Get Curious! How to Save Your Marriage from "Communication Problems" and Live Happily Ever After.*

Here's a sample of what you'll find in the book . . .

CHAPTER TWENTY-THREE

"Don't Get Mad... Get Curious!"
How to Save Your Marriage from "Communication Problems" and Live Happily Ever After

(Sample Chapter)

Forword

"Happily Ever After?" Is That Even POSSIBLE?!"

As you already know if you've read my companion book, *Date Your Mate: How to Save Your Marriage from the Blahs and Live Happily Ever After*, the answer to that question is an emphatic "Yes!"

Decades of research have made it clear: not only are there many, many couples living happily ever after "under the radar" right now, but even better, it isn't hard to do. You just need to do a few simple things that most couples don't do.

I've spelled out how to do many of those "few simple things" in *Date Your Mate*, and I'd actually suggest you read that book first, before you read this one. That's because until you've built the positive foundation you will learn how to build in that book—it's easy and fun, I promise!—you are likely to find it a lot harder to use what you will learn in this book to make your relationship better.

This book is designed to help you tackle more gracefully the tougher challenges that will probably remain even after you've started feeling enough better about each other and your relationship to begin living happily ever after.

What you will learn in this book

- Once you've put the sparkle back in your relationship and built a reservoir of good feeling, you'll trust each other enough and feel good enough about each other to be able to address the *"irreconcilable" differences* that destroy so many relationships.

- You'll learn *a new way of listening* to each other that is a lot easier and works much better than trying to "repeat back to the other person what he or she is saying." (In fact, you'll learn why trying to use communication techniques like "repeat back what you heard the other person saying" is often the WORST thing you can do!)

- You'll learn *the three biggest mistakes* that are most likely to lead to divorce—and how you can do what the couples who live happily ever after do instead.

- You will finally learn how to *get through to each other* so you can deal with *lingering dissatisfaction*—the things your partner keeps doing (or not doing!) that keep driving you crazy and can suck all the positive feeling back out of your relationship.

- You'll learn what to do when you and your partner want different, incompatible things. You'll learn how to use the Conflict Transformer™ to *transform conflict into closeness* instead of letting it tear your relationship apart.

And what if you get all the "junk" out of your relationship so your relationship gets to the point where it feels "nice"... but BORING? What if you begin to feel stuck, to feel that your relationship isn't going anywhere—or that you aren't going anywhere in your life?

- You'll learn how to help each other to *release the energy* trapped in shadows from the past or in unexplored dreams for the future—how to take your relationship to a level of intimacy, mutual support, love, and satisfaction most couples don't even know is possible.

Sound good? Let's get started!

(To be continued in
"Don't Get Mad . . . Get Curious!" . . .)

To get a special bonus when you buy
"Don't Get Mad. . . Get Curious!"
How to Save Your Marriage from "Communication Problems"
and Live Happily Ever After,
go to www.drkonline.com/dymbonus

(Your Notes):

What will you do to bring more happiness to your relationship?

(Your Notes)

(Your Notes)

(Your Notes)

(Your Notes)

(Your Notes)

(Your Notes)